Tony Manning

"I frequently refer to my interactions with Tony M – refuelling my tank.' His ability to understand business issues we are dealing with, yet keep us sustain us in the future, is remarkable."

– Len Fantasia, Vice President,
Quality & Compliance Services Worldwide,
Johnson & Johnson

Making Sense of Strategy

"*Making Sense of Strategy* is a brief but highly useful discussion of modern strategic management from the perspective of an experienced practitioner. Tony Manning is able to take many commonly held ideas in strategy and weave them into a simple, yet elegant tapestry for appreciating the art of management ... The book is recommended for MBA programs, especially executive MBA programs, and all managers who doubt their impact on the long-term success of the firm. For anyone wishing to make an organization more effective, reading *Making Sense of Strategy* will be an hour well spent."

– Jeffrey P. Katz, *Academy of Management Executive*

"Good strategy is based on only a few principles and Manning has captured them all. The shortest strategy read available, yet still comprehensive. The perfect companion for the busy executive."

– Professor Andrew Campbell, Director,
Ashridge Strategic Management Centre, London

Discovering the Essence of Leadership

"The book is an astonishing mixture of inspiration and practical business advice ... It is the finest work available for the busy businessperson who wants to get to grips with the subject." – Wessel Ebersohn, *Succeed*

competing through
value
management

competing through
value
management

TONY MANNING

ZEBRA

Published by Zebra Press
an imprint of Struik Publishers
(a division of New Holland Publishing (South Africa) (Pty) Ltd)
PO Box 1144, Cape Town, 8000
New Holland Publishing is a member of Johnnic Publishing Ltd

First published 2003

10 9 8 7 6 5 4 3 2 1

Publication © Zebra Press 2003
Text © Tony Manning 2003

All rights reserved. No part of this publication may be reproduced, stored in a retrieval system or transmitted, in any form or by any means, electronic, mechanical, photocopying, recording or otherwise, without the prior written permission of the copyright owners.

PUBLISHING MANAGER: Marlene Fryer
MANAGING EDITOR: Robert Plummer
COVER AND TEXT DESIGNER: Natascha Adendorff
TYPESETTER: Natascha Adendorff

Set in 10 pt on 14 pt Palatino

Reproduction by Hirt & Carter (Cape) (Pty) Ltd
Printed and bound by Paarl Print, Oosterland Street, Paarl, South Africa

ISBN 1 86872 673 8

www.zebrapress.co.za

Log on to our photographic website www.imagesofafrica.co.za for an African experience

*For Sandy and Lee,
the loves of my life*

CONTENTS

INTRODUCTION	11
A new agenda	13
The value imperative	14
The building blocks	15
Introducing the ValuePlan	17

1 THE NEW CONTEXT — 19
- Blinding optimism — 20
- Eden for entrepreneurs — 20
- No limits to growth — 22
- Wake-up call — 23
- Back to earth — 24
- The rise of value-based management — 26
- No panacea — 28
- Where the rubber meets the road — 29
- The reality of strategy — 31
- It's not about numbers — 31

2 WHAT VALUE MANAGEMENT MEANS — 33
- The quest for "value" — 34
- Living in harmony — 36
- First among equals — 36
- Meaningful goals — 38
- Investment and enterprise — 39
- Earning the right to grow — 41
- The perils of success — 42
- The performance challenge — 43
- Beating the commodity trap — 45
- The innovation you need — 47
- Your "right" customer — 48
- Trade-offs — 50
- Slogans aren't enough — 52
- A costly disconnect — 53
- Declare war on confusion — 54
- Hard work ahead — 56

3 THE PROCESS — 57
- A broad-brush view — 58
- Your difference matters — 61
- Keep it simple — 62
- A context for action — 63
- Strategic conversation — 65
- Crafting the message — 66
- Cascade the energy — 68
- 30-day deadlines — 69
- Definition of a value driver — 71
- Your ValuePlan must fit — 72

4	**WHAT GETS MEASURED ...**	**73**
	Needed: a holistic view	75
	Managing expectations	77
	Beyond the numbers	79
	The best tools for the job	82
	The importance of assumptions	84
	The trap of too much information	85
5	**MONEY MATTERS**	**88**
	No certainty	89
	The trouble with accounting	90
	You can only count (on) cash	94
	The cost of capital	96
	From intentions to action	97
	Choosing your "hill"	99
	Principles before precision	100
	Training and communication	101
6	**MAKING IT WORK**	**104**
	Possibilities ahead	104
	Be specific about where you start	105
	First, shed flab	107
	Sell! Sell! Sell!	109
	Get the best price	110
	Opportunity search	111
	The next 30 days	112
7	**MANAGEMENT MUST MANAGE!**	**124**
	The people factor	125
	Value and values	126
	Context and content	127
	One step at a time	127
	Maintaining momentum	129
	The cycle of success	129
	CONCLUSION	**133**
	A journey of growth and renewal	134
	REALITIES	136
	READING	138
	REFERENCES	140

INTRODUCTION

> *"We are not trying to split the atom, perform genetic recombination, or explore the solar system. All that may be required is to return to basics, to ask what makes sense and what is important for the organization: What information is needed for management planning and control functions?"*
>
> H. Thomas Johnson and Robert S. Kaplan, *Relevance Lost*, 1987[1]

Here's a bet: your company is not firing on all cylinders. You're not delivering the results that are possible. You're not getting the most from your assets. Your stakeholders aren't all as satisfied as they could be. Competitors are taking away your customers and profits.

In short, *you are destroying rather than creating value.*

How do I know?

Because I'm told so by people at all levels in almost every firm I work with. The evidence is there in media reports, in stock market indices, and in customers' comments on radio talk shows. Not a day goes by without a long list of firms getting into trouble or going bust. Not a day passes without prominent executives biting the dust.

Recently, I lectured on strategy to a business school class of mid-level managers. After I'd showed them how to put together a plan, and underscored the importance of selling it to everyone, one woman called me aside.

"How do we get this message to our bosses?" she asked. "I'm sure they have a strategy. But we just don't know about it. They want us to be innovative and to show initiative, but we're working in the dark."

As are most people in most organizations. There's hidden value everywhere.[2]

If you don't believe it, try this test:

1. Do all members of your team understand your firm's strategy, and their role in making it happen?
2. Is everyone pulling in the same direction?
3. Are they all focused on the few actions that will make the greatest impact on your results?
4. Have they been trained and equipped to do their jobs properly?
5. Are they actually *doing* the right things – and in the best possible way?
6. Does your management style inspire them to discover their true potential?

Before you say yes to all these questions, consider four others:
7. Are your efforts concentrated on your "right" customers?
8. Is your value proposition as sharp as it could be for them?
9. Is your business model customized to meet their needs?
10. Are you measuring the right things in the most practical way, and are you learning from your results?

Now here's a prediction: if you keep looking where you've been looking for ways to improve your performance, you'll never be satisfied. Odds are you think this is about numbers. Well, it's not. It's about people.

I've been consulting to big companies in most industries for many years. Here's a composite snapshot:

> **Because managers are unclear about what they must do and how to do it, they set their people up to *destroy* rather than *create* value.**

A firm's performance depends 100 per cent on its people. By now, everyone agrees they're "our most important asset." The best leaders know that their Number One job is to create "a community of champions."

So how might you do that? What *should* you do, starting today, to make every one of your people as great as they can be?

"One should always ask: What is the simplest method that will give us adequate results?" says Peter Drucker. "And what are the simplest tools?"[3]

Fortunately, there are simple methods and simple tools. Although the world is a confusing place, and although there's no denying that management is a complex, perplexing task, much of what you need to do is not difficult. Sure, it might take some hard work. And, yes, you might initially have an uphill battle getting everyone to buy in to what you're doing. But that doesn't take away from the essential point. You'll get radically improved results if you just apply some common sense and discipline.

Here's how:
- Simplify everything (I'm going to keep saying this);
- Focus on the basics;
- Do a few right things rather than lots of wrong ones;
- Put one building block in place at a time;
- Craft and conduct a strategic conversation that keeps all your people "in the loop" all the time;
- Push the limits of performance – and keep pushing.

It's unclear whether companies fail mostly because of poor *strategy* or poor *execution* of strategy. What is clear is that the best strategy in the world is useless if you can't turn it into action.

Many firms would do better with new strategies. Almost all firms would do better if they honed their ability to *execute*. This will be the battlefield of the twenty-first century.

A new agenda

The world has suddenly become a very different arena for business. Now, more than ever, executives have to be value creators.

The firms of the future will be those that do most for all their stakeholders.

They will be leaders in creating shareholder wealth, in competing for customers and serving them, in caring for their people, and in supporting their communities. They will be good citizens of the countries where they operate. Their corporate governance practices will be exemplary. Their ethics will be beyond reproach.

This new agenda applies equally to large and small firms, to publicly owned ones and to those in private hands. It applies to companies in every industry, in pretty well every country.

But how on earth can you do all this? Isn't such a complex agenda beyond even the most capable executives and the most remarkable companies?

Sure, it's a stretch. But it's also reality. If you're tempted to say, "That's not for me," then business is not for you.

But, as with much in life, you have a choice: you can make things complex or you can make them simple.

This small book takes the second course. It offers a way to make good things happen.

It's ambitious in its scope, and particularly so given its brevity. But together with my two earlier books, *Making Sense of Strategy*[4] and *Discovering the Essence of Leadership*,[5] it provides all the tools you need.

The starting point and the underlying theme is value-based management (VBM). *Competing Through Value Management* is about how you and your team can shape your strategy and identify the actions that will create real value. It's about how you can cut waste and get "the most bang for your bucks." It's about how to energize your entire organization. And it's about doing the things today that will ensure that your company doesn't just *survive* over the long term, but also *outperforms* your competitors to become increasingly valuable to all stakeholders.

The value imperative

Companies can do three things to create more value for shareholders (and thus for other stakeholders):
1. Reorganize their portfolio of business activities (the firms they own, their lines of business);

2. Restructure their finances;
3. Improve their use of assets.[6]

The first option applies mainly to large firms, and especially to conglomerates. These are also the organizations for which the second option, financial engineering, is likely to be attractive. Both tasks rest mainly with a few senior executives. Neither is likely to be ongoing.

Better asset use applies to everyone in every company. There's no end to the process. It has to be the focus of most managers. So it's the focus of this book.

The building blocks

Improving business performance is very big business. A huge amount of research goes into trying to learn what separates winners from also-rans. We know a great deal about many aspects of management that is of immense value.

Yet, when the conversation turns to "delivering value" – the issue on which all else turns – we come up short. Our toolkit is cluttered. A lot of the tools are very old.

We still use a bookkeeping system cooked up by a Venetian monk, Fra Pacioli, about 500 years ago. "Economic profit" or "residual income," one of today's favourite concepts, was talked about by economists in the 1890s, tested by General Motors in the 1920s, and further refined by General Electric in the 1950s and 1960s. The Du Pont system (which we'll talk about later) has been around since World War I. Management by objectives (MBO), which underpins every performance management process, dates from just after World War II.

In short, the quest for "one right way" to deliver results has not seen a huge amount of progress. Or, to be more accurate and less polite, it has been pretty much a dead loss.

No one will want to hear this. But perhaps if we owned up to our ignorance we'd start being more pragmatic about the task of management. A good starting point would be to consider a major study by Christopher Ittner and David Larcker, finance professors at the Wharton School at the University of

Pennsylvania, which highlights how little is known about the tools most often used in performance management efforts, and how many questions remain to be answered.[7]

Perhaps if we accepted that there's unlikely to be any major advance – certainly no glitzy new method, formula, equation, or measurement – in the next millennium or so, we'd settle down and do what we must with what we have!

Outstanding business performance depends on three very obvious – but not very common – things:
1. **Insights** – on which to base your strategy;
2. **Decisions** – about what to do;
3. **Action** – that turns your insights into results.

These, in turn, require that all your people understand not only how your firm competes, but also the impact *they* make. Then, that they know clearly what to do. And, finally, that they're empowered to make key decisions and take appropriate action.

But these are things that get said every day. So how do you close the gap between good intentions and good practice?

The quick answer: *strategic conversation*. Here's what you need to start talking about:
1. Your assumptions about the operating environment;
2. How you define your business opportunity;
3. Your value proposition;
4. Your business model design;
5. A systematic process for reviewing progress, sharing learning, and adjusting your strategy;
6. A set of metrics that will tell you how you're doing, and maybe what you should do next;
7. Rewards that will motivate people to exceptional performance.

Introducing the ValuePlan

At the risk of adding yet another acronym to the management lexicon, I refer here to *value management* (VM) rather than value-based management. It's simpler and makes the point more crisply:

> **Everything that everyone in a company does must produce value.**
> **This is an everyday process.**
> **It must become a way of thinking, a way of life.**

In the pages that follow, you'll learn about a potent idea called ValuePlanning and how to create your own ValuePlan. In brief, here's the formula:
1. Define what "value" means to your customers;
2. Identify the few drivers of that value;
3. Focus your team's attention on those drivers, and inspire them to apply their imagination and spirit where it will make most difference.

Of course, there's more to value management than this. And, of course, we'll look at other factors that make a difference. But these are the basics. Get them right, and you have a chance of success. Get them wrong, and nothing else will have the impact you hope for.

This is not a book for investors, though they might benefit from its ideas. It's not about how to value a company, though it will help you do that. It doesn't offer yet another "metric," though it does suggest ways to set goals and track performance. And although both the budgeting process and reward systems are important topics, I've given little space to them.

You won't need a consulting firm to help you apply these ideas. Nor will they take you ages to plug in.

Value management is a practical process. *Competing Through Value Management* is a working manual for managers who need to get results, and for the people who make results happen. It builds on ideas in my other books, and will equip you to design and execute a powerful new strategy.

Consultants, business school teachers, and students of management will also find this book useful. For it's based on the latest thinking from many areas of management, and also on my years of practical experience.

The principles apply to all companies. Small, privately owned firms might not have to comply with the same rules as large, listed companies, but all executives will benefit from these ideas.

Because value management is a contentious topic, especially when it comes to measurement, I've cited more sources than usual. Hopefully, I've been able to save you the time of ploughing through a very wide field, and instead let you cut to the chase with a thoroughly useful roadmap.

TONY MANNING
MARCH 2003

1
THE NEW CONTEXT

"The words, the trends, the theories change – yet the underlying tensions and themes of management remain the same."

Robert G. Eccles and Nitin Nohria, *Beyond the Hype*, 1992[8]

The last decade of the twentieth century was, for most of the world, a time of astonishing economic performance. Many countries experienced their longest, strongest growth ever. New companies, new business models, and new millionaires – and *billionaires* – popped up all over the place. Coverage of politics, sex, and scandal in the popular media gave way to news about initial public offerings (IPOs). Merger and acquisition activity went through the roof. Day traders made fortunes buying and selling shares on the Internet. I sat in one meeting in Florida where an executive used his Palm Pilot to buy and sell shares.

Technology, we were told, was driving a revolution that would run for as long as we cared to imagine. Not only did it lead to quantum improvements in productivity, it also made possible radical new ways of doing business. Transaction costs headed south. Information and money shot across the globe at "warp speed" in a "friction-free" environment. Firms unbundled their value chains. Whole industries were reconfigured as work was "disintermediated."*

When the Dow Jones Industrial Average hit 6,400 in December 1996, Alan Greenspan, chairman of the US Federal Reserve, warned against "irrational exuberance." No one took much note. The old codger usually spoke sense about the new economy, but this time he'd lost the plot.

---

* Activities were parcelled out in new ways, or in some cases abandoned entirely.

Blinding optimism

In 1999, the NASDAQ shot up by 85 per cent. Two economists, Kevin Hassett and James Glassman, wrote a book with the heady title *Dow 36,000*.[9] "Buy and hold" became conventional wisdom – after all, things could only get better, even if there was some volatility in the markets. David and Tom Gardner, founders of the funky Motley Fool investment website, told their fans that "true Rule Breakers are nearly impossible to analyze using traditional valuation criteria."[10] Smart people debated the possibility that business cycles were a thing of the past.

Nervous talk of earlier bubbles was shrugged off as unduly pessimistic and "very yesterday." Remember tulip-mania in Holland in the seventeenth century, warned the gloomsters. Remember the Mississippi Bubble in France in the eighteenth century and America's railroad boom in the 1860s and 1870s. What if it happened again?

But there were few takers for a downbeat message. Celebrity analysts saw no limits to growth. (One of the stars, Mary Meeker of Morgan Stanley Dean Witter, ranked third in *Fortune*'s 1999 list of the 50 most powerful women in American business. Abby Joseph Cohen of Goldman Sachs ranked twelfth.[11]) Scenario planners assured us we were in for a "long boom."

We were mesmerized by chaos theorists and technology gurus who talked about "increasing returns" and "network effects," and by analysts who gushed about "market space," "momentum," "eyeballs," "click-throughs," "customer lock-in." Every start-up, we were told, would be successful if the founders just "executed on their model."

Eden for entrepreneurs

US Treasury Secretary Lawrence H. Summers noted that America was the only place where entrepreneurs could "raise their first $100 million before buying their first suits."[12] It was so easy, said Jeff Bezos, the founder of Amazon.com, as he laughed his way to the bank. "They'd say, 'Here's what we're going to do, here's how it's going to work – but it only works if we get $100 million.' And people would say, 'Okay, here's $100 million.'"[13]

At the same time, reengineering was making old-style "bricks and mortar" firms lean and mean. They "hollowed out" frantically, contracting all but their core competences – preferably the really valuable "knowledge work" – to outside suppliers who were often on the other side of the world. And they invested in technology to shift "from bricks to clicks" in pursuit of lower costs and new sales.

"Telecommuting" was made easy by airlines, e-mail, and mobile phones. The "new world of work" offered flexible hours, childcare, stress counselling, aerobics classes, and classy canteens. Dressing down became fashionable. People took their dogs to the office and did skateboard tricks in the hallways. Keeping your "intellectual capital" happy was very important at a time when brain mattered more than brawn.

For a few years, it seemed as though absolutely anyone could dream up a product or service and start a business. You needed no experience, no track record, no money, and no customers. As long as you had a vision and could spin a story, that was fine.

Investors loved it. They couldn't get enough of wacky people with wackier promises. The funding industry flourished.

One venture capital firm, Accel Partners, got 10,000 business plans in 1998 – about 40 a day.[14] Altogether, VC companies put $5 billion into Internet businesses in 1998, an increase of 533 per cent from the year before. In the first three months of 1999, the amount doubled from a year back. With revenues and a growth forecast that would have made any other firm worth $3 billion, Yahoo's market cap in mid-1999 was $34 billion and its P/E ratio was an eye-popping 1,062![15]

In those halcyon days, it seemed that "new economy" companies had seized the future from the dinosaurs of the "old economy." Looking at the numbers, it was easy to know where to put your cash. You had to be mad even to consider the titans of yesteryear. Tomorrow's "knowledge" companies were on a roll, and who knew what they'd be worth in six or nine months.

The market capitalization of America Online (*before* the Time Warner deal) was worth more than GM, Ford, and the entire US steel industry combined. Red

Hat, a company that supported users of the Linux operating system, was worth more than British Airways plus Japan Airlines plus KLM.

Towards the end of 1999, the biggest concern of most managers was the threat of a "Y2K" computer glitch. So they spent fortunes to ensure it wouldn't happen – which of course pumped even more money into the tech sector and made it even more enthralling.

Some forecasters warned that after the Y2K spree, spending on technology could slow down. But everyone knew that even if there were a blip, sales would soon pick up. After all, information was critical to the functioning of every organization. Replacement cycles were shrinking. And breakthrough technologies would keep businesses forever in catch-up mode.

No limits to growth

With growth on every agenda at the century's close, companies didn't just buy whizzy new *technology*. They also bought other firms and merged with anything that moved.

In 1998, Daimler-Benz chairman Juergen Schrempp negotiated a $36-billion "merger of equals" with Chrysler, and Citicorp and Travelers got together in a $70-billion deal. In January 2000, AOL swallowed Time Warner in a $150-billion deal to create the biggest media company ever. Later that year, Vodafone AirTouch – formed in a 1998 merger worth $66.5 billion – put down $181 billion to take over Mannesmann.

According to *Newsweek*, "the sum spent on mergers and acquisitions hit a staggering peak of $3.4 trillion in 2000, when a deal was cut somewhere on the globe every 17 minutes."[16]

It seemed there was no limit to growth, no ceiling on what firms – or their CEOs – could be worth, and no distinction between bold vision and reckless megalomania. Nor were the media, investment bankers, consultants, or analysts – all of them both drivers and beneficiaries of this lunacy – of any mind to point out the realities.

For all the dire warnings, New Year's Day 2000 dawned and computers kept humming. Lifts went up and down. Water and sewage flowed. Aeroplanes took off and landed normally. Tills rang.

That February, a leader in *The Economist* began, "Another month, another record. America's expansion has just entered its 107th month, making it the longest on record."[17]

The global economy was in good shape. Nothing, it seemed, could go wrong …

Wake-up call

Good old Murphy's Law tells us that if things can go wrong, they will. And they did.

The Dow topped out at 11,723 in January 2000, and then nosedived. The NASDAQ, which had gained 85.59 per cent during 1999, peaked at 5,048 on 10 March 2000. Then it too fell – by 40 per cent in three months. Two years after its high, it was down by 75 per cent.

Other markets around the world experienced similar booms and busts. In no time at all, euphoria and blind faith gave way to panic. Within a year, $10 trillion had been wiped off global share values. By the end of 2002, the bear market had become the longest and deepest since the Great Depression.

But spreading financial gloom was just one problem facing business.

As the new century dawned, companies and their leaders found themselves under fire. Crusading writers like Naomi Klein and William Greider did a deadly job of questioning their aims, criticizing their practices, and vilifying their impact on society.

Firms like Nike and Reebok, which outsourced production work to developing countries like Mexico, Vietnam, and China, were attacked for hiring "sweat-shop" labour and paying subsistence wages.

"Globalization" became a convenient headline under which to attack any firm with international growth ambitions. At the very moment when brands were being recognized as key "invisible assets," the most valuable names of all – including Coca-Cola, McDonald's, and Shell – became lightning rods for trouble.

As protesters with the vaguest of agendas took to the streets and trashed their corporate targets, the biggest economic bust in history became more complicated. The dotcom meltdown was followed quickly by the even bigger telecommunications industry implosion. And that was followed by troubles at Enron ... Andersen ... WorldCom ... ABB ... Vivendi Universal ... Global Crossing ... Tyco ... and too many others to name.

Overnight, marquee companies everywhere fell from grace. Famous executives found themselves hauled before official hearings, doing the "perp walk," stripped of their wealth, and heavily fined. Jail terms loom for many.

Corporate governance, an issue that had been whispered about for years, suddenly became the flavour of the moment and an umbrella under which every kind of business behaviour was scrutinized, sensationalized, and criticized. "Poor governance" became code for every management misstep, and took the rap for every corporate failure.

Executive compensation, long a contentious issue, was highlighted as the cause of all kinds of misdeeds. Accounting standards were called into question, and accountants were called to account. Already frail stock markets were hurt by a crisis of confidence in corporations and those who ran them. Capitalism, it seemed, was on a knife-edge.

Back to earth

The last years of the twentieth century and the first years of the new millennium will go down in history books as an inflection point – some would say a "tipping point"* – for business. It was a sobering time.

With all that was happening, it was easy to forget why companies exist, and what makes them the most important groups in modern society. Economic realities were disregarded. The role of management became blurred. The environment became horribly confusing.

---

* Malcolm Gladwell's best-selling book, *The Tipping Point* (New York: Little, Brown & Company, 2000), suggests that an accumulation of small events adds up, until a critical mass of energy causes things to "tip."

Yet there should be no doubt at all about the place of businesses and their executives:

> **Companies are money machines. They are there to produce more wealth than they use. All their other goals – and there may be many – matter only insofar as they contribute to this one** (Figure 1-1).

Figure 1-1: *A business is a money machine*

When a budding entrepreneur thinks about starting a business, one question ranks above all others: "Will doing this produce more money than it costs?" If the answer is no, and that person elects to go ahead anyway, they probably have a charitable or ideological motive – plus more money than they need.

When investors put money into a company, they're more specific. They want to know, "*How much* will I get back? *When* will I get it? What's my *risk*?"

All other stakeholders rely on a firm being profitable. For only when it is can it buy goods and services, employ people, pay taxes, fund social programmes, and so on.

This should be obvious. But managers everywhere wrestle with questions like these:
- What is our purpose?
- Which stakeholders matter most?
- What's the best way to measure our performance?
- What must we improve, and how can we do it?

Privately held companies are likely to be run by their owners. Often these are the founders or their family members. There may also be other shareholders. In some cases, everyone might get on quite well and agree on strategy; in others, relationships may be feisty or even downright poisonous.

Public companies tend to be run by hired guns who may or may not own shares. These firms have many shareholders, with differing agendas. Some might be individuals. Some might be major institutions, investing on behalf of *their* investors. Each of them has their own expectations, and each can exert different degrees of pressure on management.

Yet, while private and public firms are clearly different, both need to:
1. Give all stakeholders the "value" they seek;
2. Align the interests of owners and managers;
3. Incentivize management and employees to work as a team for optimum results.

Doing these three things has always been important. Today, it's a matter of utmost urgency. And there's help at hand.

The rise of value-based management

The last decade of the twentieth century saw a boom in the marketing of management ideas. Yet, as I've noted, not many were new. For all the talk of the need for innovation in business, there was surprisingly little innovation when it came to management itself. But a shortage of substance didn't deter anyone. Snappy titles, glossy packaging, and brash promotions created a market.

Managers, always on the lookout for ways to grow their companies and profits, tried everything. They reengineered the fat from their firms. They crafted sexy new mission statements, became champions of six-sigma quality, talked knowledgeably about knowledge management, and committed themselves to "surprising and delighting" their customers.

In the good times, few people tried to check whether all this newfangled stuff did what it was supposed to. Business was on a high. There was so much to do and so little time.

As an article in the *Financial Times* notes, managing a big firm is easier when stock prices are soaring. After all, "Who needs organic growth when acquisitions can be financed with highly rated paper? Who needs corporate culture when employee loyalty can be bought with stock options? Who needs to make profitable investments when investors are interested only in growth?"[18]

But with hard times here, and with some observers suggesting that we could be in a 10- to 20-year bear market, executives need to rapidly pull their heads out of the clouds (or wherever else they might be) and get their feet back on the ground.

The sudden onset of a growth and profit squeeze has changed everything. Now, managers are grasping eagerly for a set of tools that will actually deliver *results*. And with such a juicy business opportunity in prospect, there are plenty of "experts" lined up with fancy new tools to sell.

For consulting firms, helping companies measure and manage performance is a cash cow. They each offer their own proprietary approaches to areas like strategy, people management, manufacturing, and supply chain operations. So it wasn't a big jump to branding and promoting their performance management "solutions" under the generic label of value-based management.

Thirty years ago, "management by objectives" (MBO) was the rage, and executives were guided by accounting measures such as return on investment (ROI). Now, "balanced scorecards" are hugely popular, and "economic profit"* is touted as the ultimate test of performance.

---

* The formula: net operating profit after taxes (NOPAT) – cost of invested capital.

Stern Stewart's economic value added (EVA™) is a highly regarded approach. McKinsey measures free cash flow. Holt Value Associates advocates cash flow return on investment (CFROI). The Boston Consulting Group uses cash value-added (CVA) and total business return (TBR). Marakon likes total shareholder return (TSR). A.T. Kearney punts operational asset effectiveness (OAE). And there are many others in the "metrics wars."[19]

Each of these methods and measures has its critics and its fans. All have advantages, but none is perfect. What works for one management team will grate with another. Choosing between them isn't easy. It's made harder by consultants sniping at each other's methodologies, and by academic researchers who highlight the flaws in every offering.

However, the differences between branded approaches are less significant than the similarities. They all have four things in common:
1. They're based on *economic* rather than *accounting* profit (i.e., they recognize the cost of capital used in delivering value);
2. They're less easy to apply than they're made out to be;
3. It's not clear that they lead to improved business results;
4. Their link with stock prices is tenuous.[20]

No panacea

If you think a clever acronym or a few new metrics will cure all your corporate ills, forget it. Every consulting firm warns potential clients that implementing value management takes time and a lot of effort. Results, they say, should not be expected for four to six months in small firms, and three to five years in big ones. Progress involves a series of difficult steps.

Not everyone is convinced it's worth the effort. Consider these words of caution:
- According to John D. Martin and J. William Petty, authors of *Value Based Management*, "recent studies of the long-term performance of firms that adopt VBM do not document significant differences in the performance of the adopting firms and similar nonadopters." The two Babson College

- professors go on to say that "things might have been worse if the firms had not adopted VBM." But of course there's no way to know.[21]
- Writing in the *Harvard Business Review* (July–August 2001), Philippe Haspeslagh, Tomo Noda, and Fares Boulos warn against the seductive "theoretical simplicity" of value-based management. Their research shows that *"almost half the companies that have adopted a VBM metric have met with mediocre success"* (my italics).
- Research shows that as many as 40 to 50 per cent of firms that try value-based metrics give up the effort in three to five years (just when they should be seeing some benefits). Those that claim to stick with the process may in reality just hang on to the name, but change their approach.[22]

Why these bleak views?

One clue lies in the fact that most of the failures "focus their programs almost entirely on changing their accounting and control systems."[23]

But that's not what value management is about. That's like trying to make your car go faster by installing a new speedometer. It won't work. Neither will it help to get a new oil gauge or odometer.

You need to tune the engine or replace it. You also need to work on all the supporting systems – electronics, power train, gearbox, suspension, braking, steering. And, after all that, you might need driving lessons. Or possibly a new driver. Or even a new car!

Where the rubber meets the road

Value management, like all other business "tools," *depends for its effectiveness on the people who use it*. It has to answer a simple question for everyone:

"What the hell must *I* do on Monday morning?"

This is especially true outside of the CEO's office – which is usually "where the action is." Translating a big picture view of strategy into a "to-do" list for individuals far down the line is always hard. Sophisticated metrics and complex implementation processes don't help.

Through no fault of their own, most people in most companies haven't a clue what their firm's strategy is or what it means to them. This is a *management* problem. That it exists should be no surprise at all.

A large number of senior executives don't know where value is created or destroyed in their firms.[24] How, then, can anyone else know what to do? The multiplier effect of this ignorance is more than any company can afford.

Stefan Reichelstein, professor of accounting at the Stanford Graduate School of Business, cites research suggesting that one in five of the *Fortune* 1000 use some kind of value-based measure to assess the performance of their top managers.[25] Given the importance of this issue (and the noise about performance-related pay in the media), this is a remarkably small number.* The obvious and alarming implication is that *most people in most of those organizations – and probably in most organizations altogether – are carelessly tracked, if at all, in terms of the value they add.*

You may think this odd, given the importance of doing it and doing it well. After all, by now everyone knows that "what gets measured gets managed."

But face it: managers have little staying power when it comes to business tools. They chop and change frenetically. They try something for a while, but waver when their people argue against it or just don't go along. They discover that it chews up time and effort, yet doesn't quite work for them or has unintended consequences, so they drop it and try something else. And, of course, the more they chop and change, the more they confuse everyone, and the less progress they make.

Perhaps even worse, they also confirm that they don't know what they're about and can't be relied on to follow through. This, in turn, destroys trust and leads to all kinds of toxic behaviours. The "I told you so" brigade has a field day.

Compared to a lot of other tools, VM as it is commonly sold is particularly tricky. It touches on literally everything a firm does, which means there's plenty

---

* Adding up the number of firms consultants say they've sold on VBM suggests many more users, but fails to account for "churn" as clients drop the process.

of scope for it to come off the rails. But the need for it is compelling. So the need for a simpler route is equally necessary.

The reality of strategy

The world is a tough place for everyone. We're now well into a new era of hostile competition. Like every other period, it'll have its winners and its losers.

Few firms have run out of growth opportunities. Most are held back not by what happens *outside* their walls, but by what happens *inside*.

The essence of strategy is to make a difference that matters. Ideally, companies should aim to do this over time – in other words, to create a *sustainable* competitive advantage. But in today's hyper-competitive environment it's hard to stay ahead for long. So while you may be able to *outsmart* your competitors in the short term, it might be more important to *outrun* them in the long term.

Obviously, though, you should strive to win on both counts: to create a better strategy *and* to execute it better than others can do. Pull that off, and you'll have a long and profitable future!

It's not about numbers

Business leaders imagine that they can take their firms to new heights by making a few cold decisions. They think that if they choose the right metrics, measure performance against them, and pay their people accordingly, everyone will act like an owner. Hard work, teamwork, responsibility, honesty, loyalty, and other good things will automatically follow.

These assumptions are baseless and the cause of a great deal of trouble.

While a company is a money machine, it is first and foremost a *human community*. Its most important work is not buying, selling, or making stuff, but *managing relationships*.

There's no doubt that many companies would do better with a better set of metrics. But nor can there be any doubt that most executives go overboard in their efforts to control things.

They measure too much – and usually the wrong things. They use metrics that don't work for them. They pour resources into capturing and analysing information. Then they share it selectively, on a "need to know" basis, or distort it to suit their political ends. And, after all that, they change nothing.

Often, the people around them don't understand the information that's available. Or they distrust it. And they too twist and slant it – or bury it – to suit their own ends.

In reality, many employees – perhaps most of them in companies of any size – will never act like owners. The only reason that *some* may is that you treat them as human beings – with respect and integrity.

Metrics can make a difference. So can financial rewards. But neither will cause ordinary people to do extraordinary things for long.

Remember this when you begin your value management journey. Come back and remind yourself of it when you hit bumps in the road.

2
WHAT VALUE MANAGEMENT MEANS

"Leaders in an execution culture design strategies that are more road maps than rigid paths enshrined in fat planning books."

Larry Bossidy and Ram Charan, *Execution*, 2002[26]

Let's begin at the end – because that's where you've got to get to.
- The first executive function, said Bruce Henderson, founder of the Boston Consulting Group, "is preservation of the organization."[27]
- Corporate executives, observe Gordon Donaldson and Jay Lorsch of the Harvard Business School, "are primarily concerned with long-term corporate survival."[28]

Preservation. Survival. Hardly exciting, but hard to argue with. Particularly since most start-ups die within five years and few firms last more than 40 or 50 years. (A study cited by *The Economist* found that the life expectancy of the average Japanese and European firm was less than 13 years!)[29] The job tenure of CEOs is falling fast.

Durable companies are few and far between. Dead companies are no use to anyone. Staying in business is a very big deal. So *the fundamental task of a leader is to produce the results that will keep their company alive.*

But it's not enough that you can merely feel a pulse.

Companies that cling to life aren't attractive to anyone. They may linger for a long time, and be admired for their longevity. But they can't fulfil their economic or social obligations.

As their competitiveness is blunted, the cost of keeping them on life support becomes unjustifiable. Attracting and keeping customers gets costlier and more difficult. The best people no longer want to work there. Suppliers don't seek their business. Other stakeholders get restive.

As important as it is to survive, however, companies need a larger goal.

- "A firm's capacity for growth has important influence on its survival," says Amar Bhidé, a Harvard Business School academic.[30]
- "Like all organisms," says Arie de Geus, formerly worldwide planning co-ordinator at Royal Dutch/Shell, "the living company exists primarily for its own survival and improvement: to fulfill its potential and to become as great as it can be."[31]

Growth. Improvement. Potential. Now we're getting somewhere. These are matters of utmost importance to any living thing. They're also ambitions that give meaning to work, and that most people are likely to sign up for.

When managers are given stewardship of a company, they surely have an obligation to make it all it could be rather than to settle for mediocrity. They need to test themselves – and be tested – against this question:

> **Do we deliver as much value from the assets entrusted to us as the best performer in the world could do?**

If the answer is no, they need to reconsider what they're about. For stakeholders are being short-changed if someone else could do better with the same capital, people, ideas, patents, brands, plant and equipment, or distribution channels. Managers are squandering precious resources. And that can't continue forever.

The quest for "value"

"Value" is a favourite word in business. "Adding value" has become a synonym for almost any work. Every job-seeker boasts about their ability to "add value." Most products and services promise "added value." And of course, VM has become a hot management fad.

But what is "value"? Who judges it to be so? Whose opinion matters most?

And how can a company *add* value without incurring extra effort or costs that, perversely, *subtract* value from its own bottom line?

VALUE?

Begin with how different people view "value":
- To *customers*, value is a perceived level of quality or performance at an acceptable price;
- To *shareholders*, value is a real financial return;
- To *employees*, value is a secure job, income, training and development, respect, social contact, and the prospect of doing something worthwhile;
- To *suppliers*, value is regular orders, satisfied buyers, ideas for improvement, few hassles, and payment without delay;
- To *society*, value is a clean environment, jobs, and support for healthcare, welfare, education, the arts, and sport;
- To *government*, value is taxes, job creation, training, and social services and support.

"Value" is not the same thing to everyone. We all interpret it differently. What's "value" to one stakeholder is unimportant to another. What one buyer will pay a premium price for is taken for granted by another. Beauty really is in the eye of the beholder.

This means that *it's the beholder's perception of value that matters most*. Your opinion doesn't count for much. So put yourself on the receiving end. The deeper your understanding of your stakeholders' expectations, values, beliefs, goals, and intentions, the better your chances of moving ahead in partnership with them.

Hard data can produce valuable insights. But less tangible perceptions and impressions often matter even more. *Facts* help us make up our minds. But *feelings* tip the scales. Logic tells a story about what, how, when, and where. But intuition reveals "the reason why."

Living in harmony

Companies have many stakeholders, each with their own view of what's acceptable and right. Growing numbers of activists demand attention for their causes. It's only logical that current thinking in corporate governance should emphasize the "triple bottom line" – shareholders, society, and environment. (Or, as Royal Dutch/Shell puts it, "people, planet, profits.")

To some managers, all stakeholders are a nuisance to be humoured and outdone in a battle of wits. They think about customers one *transaction* at a time, and aim to screw maximum returns for themselves from every deal. And they're equally expedient when it comes to employees, investors, suppliers, and all the rest.

Enlightened executives know this is a short-term attitude. They understand that *relationships* are their most valuable assets, and that only by building deep, enduring bonds can they expect a long-term flow of revenues – and thus real corporate wealth.[32]

In the years ahead, more companies will get the message. Either they'll do it voluntarily, or they'll be forced to accept reality. *Business is a cooperative venture*. You can't go it alone in the global marketplace and hope to win.

Symbiosis – living in harmony with the world around you – is more than just a feel-good attitude. It's a fundamental factor in your firm's survival and growth.

First among equals

As important as all stakeholders are, no business person should be in any doubt: *shareholders come first*. The interests of other stakeholders must be managed *to create shareholder value*.

Not everyone wants to hear this. It goes down better in the US, for example, than in Europe. There's a risk that emphasis of the "triple bottom line," now fashionable in debates about corporate governance, will cause shareholder primacy to be watered down.

But managers should understand the consequences.

There appears to be a distinct link between an *explicit commitment* to shareholder value and *effective implementation* of value management. Firms making such commitments also report improvements in their share prices. Those whose commitment is *implicit*, or that adopt a balanced stakeholder approach, do less well.[33] You ignore this reality at your peril.

Let me put that another way:

> **If you make it clear that you aim to deliver value to *all* your stakeholders, but that shareholder wealth is your No. 1 goal, you'll be most likely to satisfy everyone who matters and drive up your share price.**

The business of business is *business*. By focusing on creating value for shareholders, firms can also create value for other stakeholders (Figure 2-1). If they put other stakeholders first, they're likely to create value for no one.

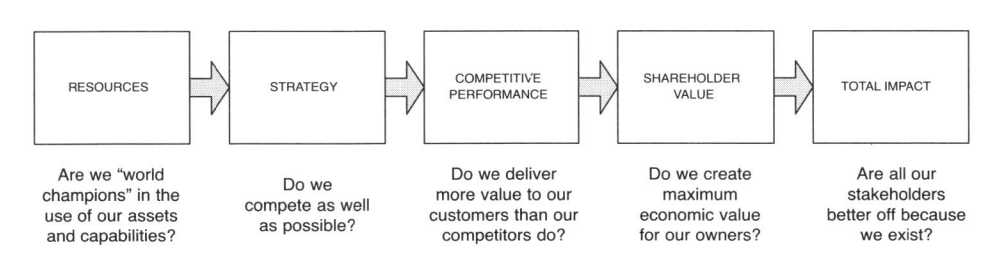

RESOURCES	STRATEGY	COMPETITIVE PERFORMANCE	SHAREHOLDER VALUE	TOTAL IMPACT
Are we "world champions" in the use of our assets and capabilities?	Do we compete as well as possible?	Do we deliver more value to our customers than our competitors do?	Do we create maximum economic value for our owners?	Are all our stakeholders better off because we exist?

Figure 2-1: *Companies must create shareholder value to create value for other stakeholders*

Meaningful goals

Top managers readily accept the need to make shareholder returns their prime concern. The need to do so is deeply embedded in the lore of business. They feel the pressure from investors. Chances are that they're rewarded for financial performance.

However, this is no guarantee that they'll make sound decisions or act in ways that will produce the expected results. In fact, commonly used metrics can encourage stupidity, selfishness, and a quest for short-term payoffs.

Most employees are unlikely to see any connection between the firm's financial goals and their work. To them, talk of EVA, profits, shareholder returns, and the like is "not my problem." It doesn't explain what they must *do*. And chances are that even if they perform well, they won't feel the benefit in their pockets or in any other way.

Drift is natural in companies. They easily gravitate to the wrong opportunities. Problems suck the life out of them. To set their course is not enough. *They must be held to it*.

Value management must be a mantra, or it'll come to nothing. It must be a board-level obsession. It must feature on every agenda and get airtime in every meeting. It must be explained, promoted, and debated at every opportunity and in every forum.

Always, though, you need to make the connection between goals, actions, and the payoff:

- For goals to be worth anything they must be meaningful – "this is *why* meeting or beating them is the right thing to do";
- People must feel that they can actually make a difference – "this is how *I* can make an impact";
- They must know what action is expected of them – "this is *what* I must do";
- And they must know what success means to them – "this is *what's in it for me*."

If your company has not delivered value in the past, that's because your people have, in effect, been trained to do something else. So to deliver value in the future, you have to re-train them.

Value management is, at its core, about communication. It's a tool that enables leaders to explain where a firm is headed, how it'll get there, and who must do what to make it happen. Understand this, and you have a head start in the race for tomorrow's customers and profits. Ignore it or forget it, and you will be road kill.

Investment and enterprise

"Enterprises are paid to create wealth," says Peter Drucker, "not control costs."[34] Growth doesn't come through cost-cutting. Growth requires investment.

In a perfect world, managers would watch costs religiously, and spend only for growth. But the world is not perfect, and waste is a reality. If costs are not deliberately controlled, they rise by default.

It might be critical, at various stages in the evolution of a firm, for managers to take a particularly hard line on costs. Sooner or later just about every company hits a rough patch. But occasional slashing is no substitute for constant vigilance and control. Desperate measures are bad for morale. Besides, they're *reactive*, and not part of a long-term strategy.

The purpose of performance management and incentive schemes is to encourage executives to be proactive, and to do what's good for growth. Yet the measures that firms apply often have precisely the opposite effect.

Take return on investment (ROI), for example. To improve it, you have two choices: you can drive revenues up or costs down. You can sell more units, raise prices, or speed up your stock turn – all of which is likely to be hard work and take longer than you'd like. Or you can opt for an easier, quicker route, and cut costs. It doesn't take a genius to work out which course managers are likely to take when they're feeling the heat.

Early in the 1970s, the famous PIMS* project looked at the impact of 37 different factors on profit performance. Investment intensity was the most important determinant of ROI, after market share and product quality. In fact, the study showed "a powerful, robust, basic, negative relationship between capital intensity and profitability."[35]

The message to managers is obvious. Don't touch capital investment with a bargepole!

However, all costs are not equal. Some have a greater impact on future performance than others. It might be common sense to cut back on your stationery orders, or on flowers for the reception area. But failing to build a new plant or spend on technology upgrades can be fatal.

In a 1980 article in the *Harvard Business Review* titled "Managing our way to economic decline," Robert Hayes and William Abernathy warned that US managers "increasingly relied on principles which prize analytical detachment and methodological elegance over insight, based on experience, into the subtleties and complexities of strategic decisions."[36] This they saw as a key reason for America's loss of competitiveness to Japan.

But the problem wasn't unique to *American* management. It hurt companies throughout the West. And, if anything, the problem has become more serious.

Executives everywhere are subject to the same pressures and measured by the same criteria. The practice of management has become globalized. Principles taught and applied in Boston or Silicon Valley are just as popular in Durban and Dubai. Executives worldwide are soaking up and applying the same ideas.

"Managing by the numbers" is a central theme across the globe. But management is about far more than hard numbers. It's also about soft human qualities such as attitude, imagination, spirit, and ambition. It is always risky. It always involves judgement.

When a company gets into trouble, those charged with turning it around must first try to ensure its survival. Conserving resources is essential. Harsh

---

* PIMS (profit impact of market strategies) was begun in 1972 by the Marketing Science Institute, a non-profit research organization linked to the Harvard Business School.

action might be imperative. But even in the worst of times, managers must beware of cutting too deep, too fast, and maybe in the wrong areas.

No business gets to the future for free. Growth is essential for any business. But it costs money and it requires faith. You have to lay bets if you want a hope of hitting the jackpot.

Earning the right to grow

Research by Donaldson and Lorsch shows that a key driver of management behaviour is *the desire to stay independent*. They want to be able to make up their own minds about where they're taking their firms, and how – "to relax the objective constraints imposed on them; to minimize the potential for dominance by major constituencies; to increase the potential for managerial discretion; and to assure personal and corporate success."[37]

Growth is a choice, as is the manner and pace of growth. Managers can elect whether to make their companies bigger and more profitable. They can decide how to do it, and how fast. But the *right* to grow must be earned. Other stakeholders – customers and shareholders especially, but also employees, suppliers, government, and society – must come to the party.

When things go well, stakeholder support is generally easy to get. But in tough times, individual agendas get in the way. This may lead them to withhold funding, buy less, erect legal barriers, disrupt supplies, hike prices, and so on. All these moves add costs and impede value creation.

If the right to grow must be earned, it must first be *sold*. Those powerful stakeholders must know why it's a good idea. So managers must make their opportunities, goals, and strategies clear. They must do a convincing job of persuading people who see the world in a different way, and who have different needs and goals, to buy into their plans. They must explain, clearly and logically, why they deserve support.

The perils of success

When a company is near failure, it's quite easy to stir people to action. They're not stupid, and they naturally seek to avoid trouble. It's also likely that many of them aren't happy to be part of a losing team, and welcome a call to arms. So improving performance at this time is in some respects easy. Even drastic remedies can be implemented without too much argument.

Success, on the other hand, creates a trickier situation. When firms do well they're vulnerable to backsliding and decay. This happens because:
1. They become complacent. Satisfied with their results, they stop paying attention to the world around them, and lose their zest for "raising the bar."
2. As performance improves, it gets harder to improve. Diminishing returns set in.
3. The controls that they need to stay in business keep them from sensing the need for change.[38]
4. Their processes, systems, and structures become so interdependent that changing any part is difficult and risky. Unintended consequences are certain. So doing nothing looks like the safe course.
5. They suffer from what Clayton Christensen, a Harvard Business School professor, calls "the innovator's dilemma": the tendency to hone their relationships with *current* customers, while leaving themselves open to attack by competitors with inferior offerings at lower prices.[39]
6. They keep looking back at the realities they knew, rather than ahead to the possibilities they can't fully see and definitely don't understand.

One of the major challenges for any firm focusing on value management is *how to keep going*. Managers need to work hard to sustain momentum.

The good news is that for all its downsides, success does breed success. Signs of improvement enthuse people, give them confidence, and encourage them to take the next step.

These "wins" can be used to fuel ongoing change. But value managers must put in place a systematic way of identifying, publicizing, praising, and possibly rewarding progress. They must ensure that their organization learns from victory – and exploits that learning.

The performance challenge

When the economic bubble burst in 2000, executives, investors, analysts, and financial gurus woke up to a harsh fact: *long-term superior performance is a very rare thing*. Excellence occurs here and there among companies, and even then it's mostly erratic.

In a benign environment, many firms can do quite well. But when the weather turns foul, very few keep growing. Even fewer will outperform the underlying economy over time – a pathetic prospect, given that growth in developed nations is likely to be only about *two or three per cent* a year.[40]

Consider these realities*:

- According to *Fortune*, "The ultimate, pragmatic reason for not aiming at targets like 15% is the sheer difficulty – indubitable for companies of size – of growing that fast over an extended period … During a 40-year period, from 1960 to 2000, after-tax corporate profits grew at an annual rate of just over 8%."[41]
- In one of his famous letters to his shareholders, Warren Buffett, chairman of Berkshire Hathaway, wrote, "I would wager you a very significant sum that fewer than 10 of the 200 most profitable companies in 2000 will attain 15% annual growth in earnings per share over the next 20 years."[42]
- Since 1965, reports *Fortune*, "when US corporate profits peaked at 14.6% of national income, profit growth has trailed economic growth."[43]
- According to an editorial in the *Financial Times*, "As a proportion of gross domestic product, corporate profits have fallen by about a sixth in the US and a quarter in the UK. In both cases, the profit share is back at levels last seen in the early 1990s recession."[44]

---

* The first two quotes appeared in my book *Discovering the Essence of Leadership* (Cape Town: Zebra Press, 2002). I repeat them here because they are so relevant.

- In a special issue on the world economy, *The Economist* notes that in all technological revolutions, "most of the benefits of higher productivity go to consumers and workers, in the shape of lower prices and higher real wages, rather than into profits. Equity returns are therefore likely to be a lot lower over the next decade than the previous one."[45]

Right now, the consensus view of economists seems to be that the world has begun a long phase of slow growth. Uncertainties abound. Corporate profits are under pressure. Testing times lie ahead for business.

In the past decade, many business leaders made their mark through once-in-a-lifetime deals. Some built colossal businesses and produced impressive earnings growth through multiple acquisitions. Today, they're being unmasked as flash-in-the-pan performers.

With their stock prices in the tank, they can't use their cheap paper to buy companies. With the economy in a funk, organic growth isn't easy. New accounting rules and fierce scrutiny make it hard to cook the books. And volatility in the markets means there's a new demand for consistency and reliability.

Chances are that a large number of managers won't come up to expectations. Even those who did exceptionally well in the past will be hard-pressed to keep delivering.

Want proof?

Look no further than a study of 2,500 CEOs in Europe and the US, by Booz Allen Hamilton. The consulting firm found that CEOs who left for performance-related reasons actually *outperformed* their peers in the first half of their tenures. But then they hit a "significant decline" in the second half.[46]

They couldn't repeat their success. And that was in the good times. During the biggest, longest economic boom in history.

Doing something once may be easy. It might just be luck. But doing it again and again is a real test. That's what value management is for.

Beating the commodity trap

For close to 40 years after World War II, management had an easy ride. Consumer incomes rose almost everywhere and there were plenty of shoppers for just about everything. With little competition, firms could get away with shoddy quality and poor service. Workplace safety and health were of little concern. Environmentalism wasn't an issue.

Along the way, inflation became a reality in many industrialized countries. Companies seized on it to hike their prices and show impressive growth. This, in turn, provided cover for *cost* increases. So managers became careless, and their organizations became wasteful, flabby, and sluggish.

Economic theory says that in time all competitive advantages are eroded, and returns fall to zero. This happens because firms copy each other and chase the same customers – a process that's accelerated in a hyper-competitive environment.

In almost every industry today, overcapacity is giving business the blues. There's just too much on offer. At the same time, tough economic conditions have made shoppers for everything extremely cautious, price-conscious, and disloyal. The result: pricing power has evaporated, margins are slipping, and companies are struggling to sustain profit growth.

Faced with these problems, most managers instinctively cut their prices. In some circumstances, this might be a very smart emergency tactic. As a long-term strategy, however, it has severe consequences:
1. It signals to customers that you're not sure of the value of your offering;
2. It warns them you're not averse to screwing them when you can, to inflate your profits;
3. It lulls your own people into believing that there's an easy way out of a competitive bind;
4. It starts a debilitating process that's hard to stop.

If you cut prices without changing your business model, you quickly eat into profits. At the same time, aggressive competitors continue to threaten you … so customers demand still lower prices … so you have to discount even more. A few steps down this slippery slope quickly become a slide to oblivion.

Cutting prices is clearly not a sustainable strategy. If you don't cut *costs* at the same time, your margins vanish. But cost-cutting is limited by your business model. *And cost-cutting is not a recipe for growth*. Firms that rely on it quickly turn their own offerings into commodities.

What worked in the past won't work in the future. The current business environment is forcing managers to embrace sweeping changes. Ultimately, they have no choice but to rethink their strategies altogether and redesign their business models to fit (Figure 2-2).

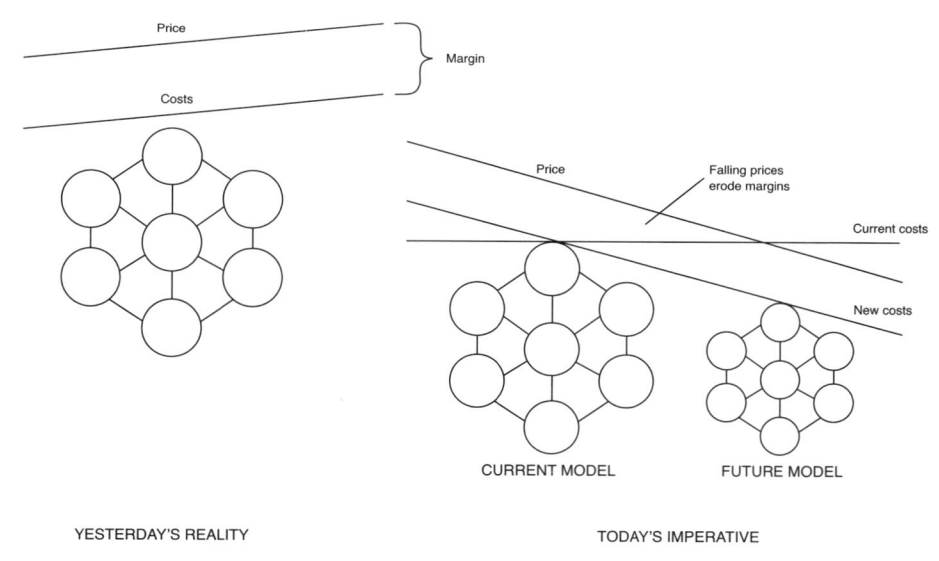

YESTERDAY'S REALITY   TODAY'S IMPERATIVE

Figure 2-2: *You may need a new business model to compete in a new arena*

The heat is on. But before you race off and turn your organization on its head, pause and think carefully about the way forward. Remember that today's assets and capabilities are your stepping stones to the future.

Very few firms need to abandon their current business models altogether, or would live to tell the tale. You might aim to do that over time, but you don't have to do it all overnight.

In most cases, *the priority is to get today's business operating as close to its potential as possible*. To "squeeze your assets" to the limit.

"If you can consistently do your work faster, cheaper, and better than the other guy," says reengineering guru Michael Hammer, "then you get to wipe the floor with him – without any accounting tricks."[47] So best you start early, and tackle the task in bite-sized chunks.

The innovation you need

Deciding when and how to change your business model demands careful thought and judgement. Should you fine-tune your current business engine, or build a new one from scratch? And when you've made this big decision, where should you start and how should you advance?

Leaders must be bold. They must also be pragmatic. They must be radical. But they must also be rational.

There are always different and better ways to do just about everything. There's always a need to challenge convention and kill sacred cows. But innovation must have a purpose. You need to be clear why you're doing it, and what results you expect. And you need some sense of where your innovation will lead – where it will take you and what you might have to do for your next act, and the one after that.

As Figure 2-3 shows, you can deliver new value by changing *direction* (a strategic choice) or improving *performance* (a process choice), or by doing both.

Every possibility involves changes in your business model. What you need to do right now might be relatively simple, and the payoff might be great. (And it always makes sense to start with the "low-hanging fruit"!) But it won't always be that easy. Nor is it smart to go the easy route when all the facts tell you that you have to make a hard call.

When your strategy is on target, the way you use your assets can make the difference that matters. So productivity improvement must always be a central theme in your value management efforts. You should set tough goals for incremental change and drive hard to reach them.

Figure 2-3: *Both strategy and execution offer competitive possibilities*

If your strategy is flawed, you face a dilemma. Should you stick with it and just try to outrun your competitors? Or should you plot a new course, design a new business model, and only then charge into battle?

Doing the wrong things the right way just gets you to the wrong place faster. Being brilliant at making stuff that no one wants is a criminal waste of resources. Ultimately, there's no escaping the need for both a sound strategy and effective operations.

In the real world, however, firms almost never have the option of doing things by the book. Instead, you have to change on the run. But that's a very good reason to know what you're trying to do and how best to go about it, to have as many of your stakeholders behind you as possible, and to break all work down into manageable pieces.

Your "right" customer

In today's competitive environment, most firms face a growing number of competitors – and increasingly hostile ones to boot. Everyone's fighting over the same bones. The only way to count for anything in the long run is to simultaneously outsmart and outpace the pack. If you relax for a moment, you'll quickly lose customers. Then, other stakeholders will follow them out of the door.

To stay in the game, you have to make a difference that matters. You have to be seen by your customers as a significant partner.

But just what does that mean? Does size count? Does market share matter?

Some people say yes. They point to the fact that virtually every sector is dominated by a few major competitors. And to evidence that you should probably rank *among the top three* in terms of market share to count for anything.[48]

But market share for its own sake is pointless – as is growth just for the heck of it. Although the famous PIMS studies of the 1970s showed a clear link between market share and profitability,[49] other evidence points to the downsides of wanting a big slice of the customer pie.[50]

For some firms the best route is not to go for more share, but rather for less. But to focus on the *right* customers, not just *any* customers.

Here's the logic:
1. Chasing customers costs money. If they don't pay you enough to make it worthwhile, and if they don't treat you as a valued supplier, catching them might prove deadly.
2. Every company has its own "right" customers. These are the ones who'll buy the most, at the highest prices, for the least possible investment of resources by you. They like your products, will pay your price, don't hassle you for service, tell everyone how wonderful you are, and keep coming back for more.
3. By focusing fanatically on your "right" customers, and by being the *world's best supplier* to them, you raise your competitors' cost of tackling them. This effectively shuts out opposition.

Growth must have a purpose. Only *profitable* growth matters.

Ultimately, there is only one way to achieve it: by being a leader in serving your "right" customer. That means you have to:
1. Pick your target carefully;

2. Create a tailored value proposition;
3. Develop an effective business model;
4. Concentrate your resources;
5. Execute meticulously (Figure 2-4).

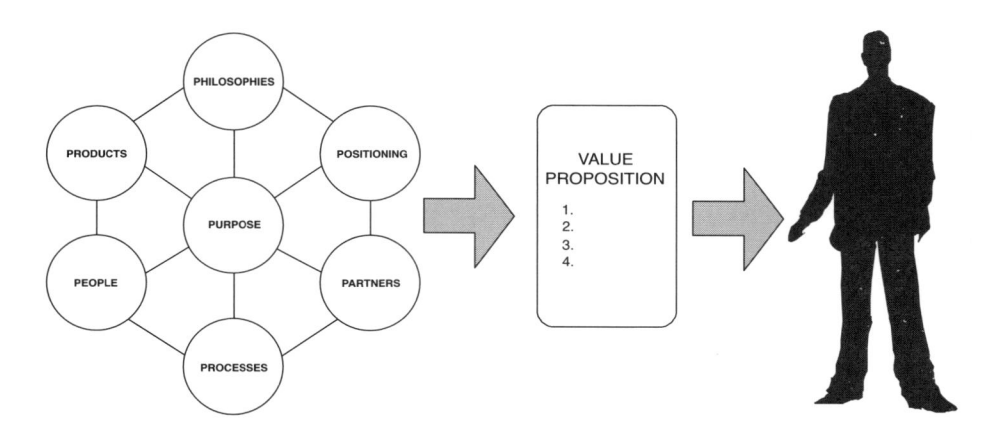

Figure 2-4: *Your business model must be designed to deliver the value proposition that's ideal for the "right" customer*

This isn't hard to grasp. Yet if you rate many firms on a 1–5 scale (where 1 is poor and 5 is excellent) on each of these tasks, they fall badly short. If your company's a culprit, improving your results shouldn't be difficult. Get these basics right, and you'll start seeing the impact fast.

Trade-offs

The business model that's designed to deliver specific value to one customer can't deliver equal value to all customers. "Spray and pray" strategies are awfully costly. As soon as you widen the scope of your appeal, you start giving some people less than they want. That leaves you vulnerable to attack by competitors who *are* focused, and whose promises are specific and tailored.

Since you can't do everything for everyone, you have to make up your mind. Only by doing so can you hope to be good enough – *to make a difference that matters* – for customers who count.

Consider what happens when you make trade-offs (Figure 2-5):

1. **You shorten your to-do list.** Managing gets simpler. You have less to do, so you can do it better.
2. **You focus your resources.** You can apply a critical mass of imagination, time, and money to your task. You can become "the world champion" at what you do.
3. **Your selling message is clear.** Your value proposition is easy to explain and easy to understand.
4. **Customers aren't forced to compromise.** They know just what to expect from you and they don't have to take second best when they buy.[51]

Every trade-off you make improves your chances of success. But the key is to make them *deliberately*; not have them forced on you, or allow them to happen by *default*.

Make trade-offs here...   ...so they're not needed here

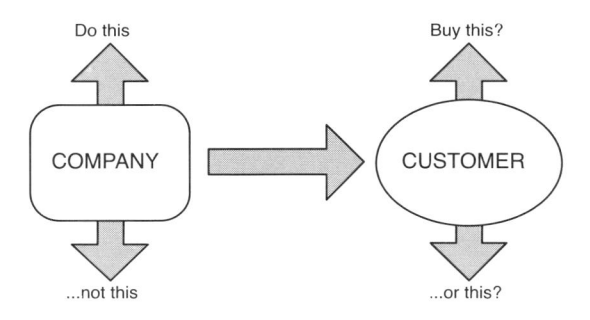

Do this   Buy this?

COMPANY ⇒ CUSTOMER

...not this   ...or this?

Figure 2-5: *The company's trade-offs eliminate the need for customers to compromise*

Obviously, there are risks. You might stop doing things that customers value. If you strip too many features or benefits from your offering – or the wrong ones – customers may dash into the arms of your competitors. By abandoning activities today, you might lose the chance to learn something that will be worthwhile tomorrow, or to build resources that will give you an edge.

As always, *balance* is the key word. But don't be immobilized by it. And don't fall into the trap of doing nothing now because you "want to keep your options open." Vagueness and value management sit uneasily together. Trying to delay the inevitable is a very bad idea.

Slogans aren't enough

Just about every company today proclaims a bold vision. Typically, they promise to be "Number One" … "the most profitable company in our industry" … "world class" … or "the customer service leader." The first thing any self-respecting executive flashes on the screen in strategy-fests is the clutch of words that's supposed to stir the troops, delight customers, make competitors quake, and win applause from government, the greenies, and the human rights crowd.

Year after year, vision and mission statements rank near the top in surveys of favourite management tools (even though they're hardly "tools").[52] Executives happily promise improved results "because we have a new mission."

But merely proclaiming your "moon shot" is just one small step in a difficult and messy journey. No amount of speechmaking will win stakeholders to your side if they don't see you walking the talk. No amount of sloganeering will take you anywhere without a solid support process. Newsletters, videos, badges, buttons, and T-shirts are a waste of money when you fail to follow through with action.

That's not to say you don't need to use every communications method available. Or that you shouldn't grab every opportunity to tell your story. After all, leadership is basically a communications task. But just as you need a good product to build a great brand, so must there be real substance behind what you say about growing your business.

A legendary advertising executive, Bill Bernbach, once warned that "a great ad campaign will make a bad product fail faster. It will get more people to know it's bad."[53] Now, be warned about your value management initiative. First, get the "product" right. Work like hell to embed it in every bone of your corporate body. Then fire up your publicity machine. And be sure to keep your promises.

A costly disconnect

Progress is only possible when you have a clear understanding of the world you're in, the pressures you face, and what you must do to make a difference that matters.

This sounds easy, but firms make heavy work of it. Their senior people cook up strategies that look great as PowerPoint presentations, but don't translate into action. There's a costly disconnect between strategy, budgeting, and front-line operations. Unacknowledged barriers keep each of these activities "in its box." Different people are responsible for each of them, and they don't talk enough to each other about their common purpose.

Too often, budgeting is the dominant process. If there's one "must do" activity in just about every firm, this is it. Because it's done annually, it serves as a useful business "kick-off." It's painfully structured, involves many people, takes lots of time, and generates piles of paper. (One study of global firms said that on average they spent more than 25,000 person-days per $1 billion of revenue on planning and measuring performance.[54])

Budgeting doesn't have many fans. The way it's commonly done, it's one of the more useless management practices. As Michael Jensen of the Harvard Business School observes, "almost every company in the world uses a budget or target-setting system that rewards people for ignoring or destroying valuable information and punishes them for taking actions that benefit the company."[55]

Yet few people doubt its importance.

Strategy, on the other hand, is a poor cousin – even though it belongs to top management. It unfolds day by day, in every part of a firm. But it gets little *formal* attention. And what it does get may be too infrequent to make a difference.

From time to time, the top team takes off to a fancy resort to do a SWOT analysis and add a few commas or adjectives to the mission statement. They come back and throw a bunch of flipchart pages to a secretary who types them up and buries them in a file. If it's been a good meeting, a few snippets of dazzling prose find their way onto the company intranet.

Meanwhile, down in the trenches, people struggle to cut costs, boost quality, leverage core competencies, reconfigure the supply chain, plug in new computer systems, develop intellectual capital, and produce balanced scorecards. They don't understand the strategy and have no "decision rights." New instructions sink beneath a flurry of existing interventions.

Many corporate activities cancel each other out. (For example, when cost-cutting eliminates jobs, it can kill any motivation to improve quality. Or efforts to fix quality may clash with others intended to improve productivity.) Zealous managers armed with the latest business tools cause terrible confusion and turf wars. Fights over resources are common. Communication breaks down, and mixed messages compound the chaos. So all in all, it's not surprising that so many companies do so badly, or that consistently great performance is so unusual.

Strategy, budgeting, and operations are all factors in a firm's success. They must be seen as contributing to each other, or they will decimate each other.

Declare war on confusion

Companies need a clear purpose. Leaders need to clearly spell out their aims and priorities, and how they see things being done. But rhetoric alone is not enough. Value management is about both relentless communication and systematic action.

Confusion is the enemy of results. The top managers of most firms have so much on their plates that they don't know what to tackle first, or what comes second or third. Because they live in a swirl of complexity, it's easy for them to see everything as complex – and to make things complex for everyone else.

One thing you can be sure of as organizations grow is that uncertainty will worsen. In no time at all, people's different world views take them down different paths. If the CEO doesn't have a clear point of view, and doesn't craft and conduct a clear and consistent strategic conversation, drift and underperformance become the norm.[56]

Outstanding executives have many strengths. Above all, they're able to simplify things for themselves and others. They cut through clutter, identify the few issues that make the most difference, and do the few things that make the greatest impact.

Strategy is basically about thinking through and debating seemingly obvious questions.[57] Most importantly, managers must consider:
- What is our business purpose?
- What are the few things we must do that will get us where we want to go?

The answers provide focus for people's efforts, and frame the ongoing strategic conversation. But to get results, you need to also consider:
- Who needs to know what, to enable us to perform?
- What must we measure to know how we're doing, and how will we do it?
- How will we use what we learn to keep moving and improving?
- How will we inspire our people to perform?
- How will we encourage other stakeholders to "vote" for us?

If you do no more than apply your mind to these issues, you'll achieve a lot. But while you're wrestling with them, you'll probably find that there's one overarching question that must be tackled:
- What is business "success"?

If it means different things to different people within your firm – and it probably does – then they'll inevitably pull in different directions. On the other hand, if they all agree what it means, they'll be able to act as one team, delivering the maximum possible value.

Hard work ahead

If there's one sure way to get your people running around like headless chickens, it's to announce, "From today, we're going to manage for value." They might nod obediently, but most will ask themselves, "What the hell does that mean? Haven't we been doing that all along?" And, more specifically, "What does it mean to *me*? How will my job change? How will this impact on my life?"

Talk is easy. Action is much harder. Doing the right things begins with careful thought about what they might be. Doing them right demands that you learn from the best sources, share information widely, and inspire the imagination and spirit of your team. It also requires a serious commitment to holding your course, the courage to say no, and the wisdom to change your mind when that becomes necessary.

You can't deliver value to your stakeholders by accident. It won't happen without trade-offs – "We must *focus on this* … we must *stop doing that*." Nor will it happen if you blithely assume, "Our people all know what to do." Or if you think that because you've empowered them, they'll do the right things in the best way.

So let's lay out a roadmap.

3
THE PROCESS

"Getting every employee's mind into the game is a huge part of what the CEO job is all about."

Jack Welch, Jack: Straight from the Gut, 2001[58]

Value management is simply a practical, disciplined way of doing business. It embraces everything from the way you lead your company to the way you make and implement strategy; from the measures you use to track your performance to how you reward your people.

Figure 3-1 shows the nine elements of the process:

1. **Leadership.** My definition of this vital role is "the achievement of a specific purpose through others."[59] Leaders create the context in which other people work. They set the goals and the pace. As we've seen in cases such as Enron and Tyco, they also set the tone.
2. **Strategy.** Decisions must be made about *where* you'll compete (which markets and customers), *what* your value proposition will be, and *how* you'll do it.
3. **ValuePlan.** A simple visual aid to help you communicate your value drivers, goals, and actions. Think of it as an "architectural drawing" for the next element, your strategic conversation.
4. **Strategic conversation.** This is the communication that sums up your strategy and keeps people focused on it. It's defined by three critical questions: *What* must we talk about? *Who's* involved? What is the *quality* of that conversation?
5. **Metrics.** How you'll measure your performance.
6. **ValuePlan forums.** A series of scheduled and carefully planned meetings in which to examine your assumptions about the environment, talk strategy, review results, and share ideas.

7. **30-day actions.** Making things happen, and making them happen fast, is a key to learning and change.
8. **Results.** To satisfy your stakeholders, you need to start with a clear picture of what they expect. Then, define what you should reasonably do for each of them.
9. **Rewards.** Most companies discover that they can make significant improvements without financial incentives. But there comes a time when people want to know, "What's in it for me?" So the reward system must be tightly tied to the ValuePlan.

As you see, there's also a feedback loop. So value management is not only a systematic way to turn your strategy into action, it's also a process of *learning* from what you do and what you achieve. It's a continual cycle of renewal. At the same time – and without any other costly intervention – it raises your "strategic IQ."

The case for involving as many of your people as possible is clear and compelling.

A broad-brush view

In *Making Sense of Strategy*, I suggested the use of a "strategy wheel" to depict the key issues companies have to manage (Figure 3-2). It offers two benefits:
1. It ensures that you consider all the factors that impact on your performance;
2. It emphasizes the fact that you have to *balance* many activities – and many competing agendas – to be successful.

The issues featured here are common to most firms. But you're free to leave some out and include others instead, if that fits your situation better. You can then decide on the most vital goals under each heading, and develop action plans to achieve them. Here are examples of what you might cover:
- **Customers** – market share, segmentation, service levels, customer satisfaction;
- **Quality** – perceptions; reject, scrap, and waste rates;

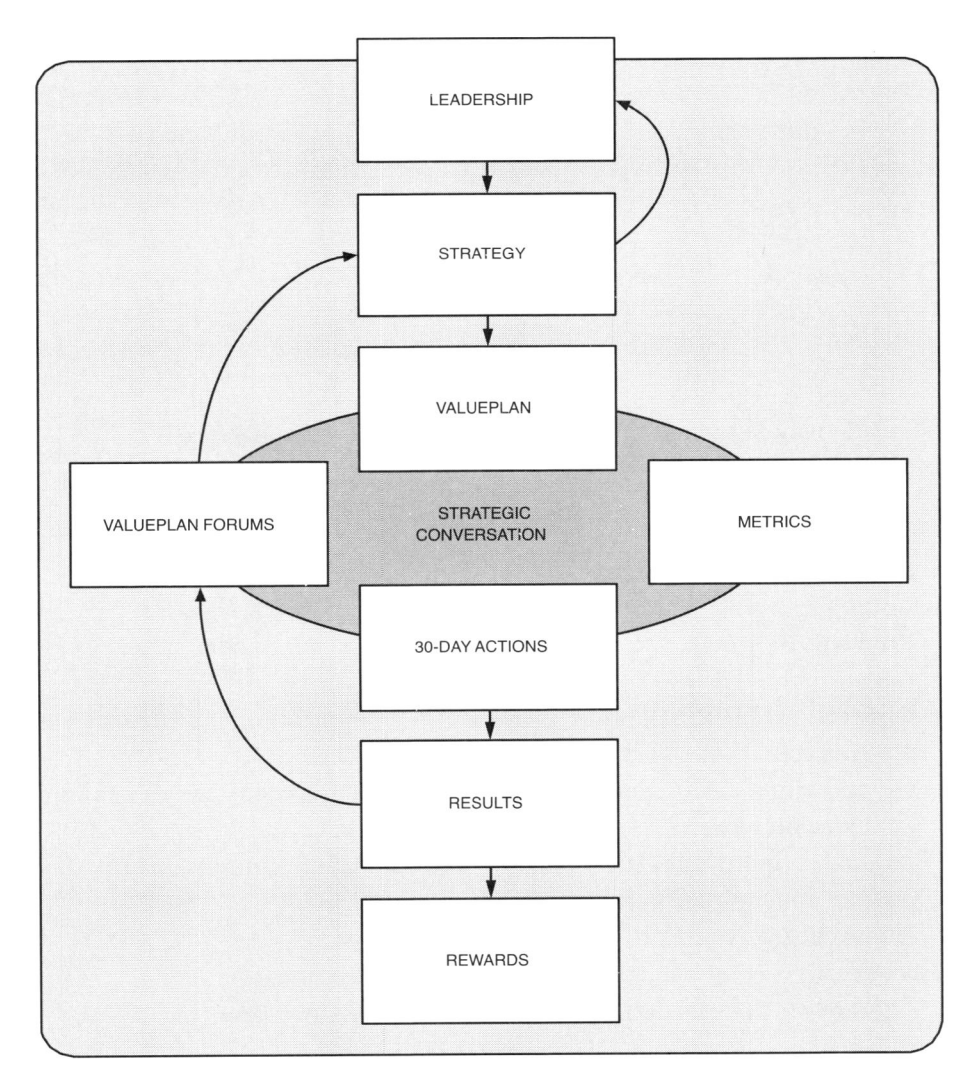

Figure 3-1: *The value management process*

Figure 3-2: *The starting point for identifying value drivers*

- **Productivity** – asset use, output per hour, output per person, improvement rates;
- **Partners** – alliances, research and development, suppliers, distributors, communities, government;
- **Organization** – structure, facilities, plant and equipment, people, training and development;
- **Product** – innovation and development, launches, concept-to-cash time, pricing, support, resale, recycling and disposal;
- **Financial** – revenues, profit, cash flow, debtors' days outstanding, investment, costs;
- **Processes** – efficiencies, cycle times, methods, technology.

But let's simplify and clarify things even further. And let's make sure that you put maximum effort and attention into the few "value drivers" that will:
- Ensure that your company survives and thrives;

- Give it a competitive advantage;
- Deliver optimum satisfaction to all stakeholders.

Your difference matters

The most popular performance management tool today is undoubtedly the balanced scorecard. Designed by Robert Kaplan and David Norton, it gives managers a balanced view of what they must work at to create value. So it has four elements: financial, customer, internal, and learning and growth.[60]

Scorecard literature suggests that all firms can use the same framework because the same four issues matter to everyone. (Details, of course, need to be specific, and will differ from company to company.)

But wait a minute. While these are important factors, they might not be ones that *all* managers need to focus on. They might matter to Company A, but not to Company B. Or they might be critical in one division of a large firm, but not to another.[61]

Results depend on getting many things right. All firms need financial goals. All firms must capture and keep customers, hone their internal processes, and keep learning and growing. But are those the issues *you* need to talk about obsessively right now? If not, what others should you include?

Every company faces unique challenges. Every company has its own history, as well as distinctive assets and capabilities. Chances are that *your* key value drivers – the ones that matter most at this stage of your company's growth – won't fit easily into those boxes.

Faced with this reality, managers are easily tempted to add more elements. According to the American Productivity and Quality Center, the average scorecard has 10 measures; some have 20.[62] This may be one reason the organization warns on its website that "as appealing and simple as it appears, implementation of the balanced scorecard has proven to be a challenge in most organizations. It is the quintessential example of the phrase 'It's simple, but not easy.'"[63]

Keep it simple

Smart CEOs know that complexity is deadly. So they do two things to ensure that the energies of their firms are focused, activities are aligned, priorities are understood, and people have an easy way to think about hard trade-offs:
1. They reduce their strategies to a few key words, ideas, or themes;
2. They "unpack" those strategies into a handful of value drivers, goals, and actions.

By cutting through clutter with messages that are simple and clear, they craft the core of their strategic conversation. This keeps agendas short and attention on the right things.

It also ensures that they can "stay on message" as they spread the word. By repeating themselves constantly, they literally drive their strategies into the DNA of their organizations. People around them not only understand them, but can also pass on the right ideas.

Here are some examples of how strategy can be distilled to its essence:
- Dell Computer's key theme is "be direct."[64]
- Wal-Mart is driven by "low prices, every day."[65]
- Southwest Airlines is a consistent profit-maker by delivering "short-haul flights at fares competitive with auto transport."[66]
- Jack Welch, the legendary former chairman and CEO of General Electric, was fanatical about keeping things simple. In the early 1980s, he urged his business leaders to make their companies "No. 1 or No. 2." In 1984 he drew three circles on a table napkin to illustrate GE's strategy. Later that decade, he introduced "Workout" to cut waste and costs. During the 1990s, "Globalization," "Services," "Six-Sigma Quality," and "e-Business" got attention.[67]
- Japanese auto-parts maker Hoyo Seiki, winner of the Deming Application Prize in 1985, uses three measures: customer satisfaction, employee satisfaction, and revenue growth rate.[68]
- Analog Devices, a semiconductor manufacturer, concentrates on just two things: customer satisfaction and new product development.[69]

- The famous Toyota Production System is underpinned by "four S's": "sweeping, sorting, sifting, and spick-and-span."[70]
- Boeing has three strategies in its "Vision 2016": "run healthy core businesses, leverage strengths into new products and services, and open new frontiers."[71]

In some of these cases, the message is core to the total organizational strategy. In others, it applies to a specific function. In every case, however, these companies are utterly single-minded, and keep things astonishingly simple. This ensures that their teams are aligned, and makes implementation effective.

A context for action

Customers wait for no one. If you don't grab them, competitors will. So you have no time to waste on "nice-to-do" stuff. The fact that we live in a 24/7 world means that in the next 24 hours – and every day after that – you have to cover ground towards your goals.

The question is:

> **What few actions are most critical to you now,
> to put you in a winning position in the future?**

One company might need to urgently train its sales force or push up its call rate. Another might have a greater need to develop and launch new products. A third might need to change its processes. There's always a small number of things that yield a disproportionate impact. The 80/20 principle is confirmed daily.

Priorities at CEO level provide a *context* for priorities at divisional or business unit level, though the specifics change in various areas. People working in the accounting office will have a different focus from those in the factory or in marketing. R&D teams must get quite different results than the buying department.

Roberto Goizueta, chairman and CEO of the Coca-Cola Company from 1981 to 1997, was one of the all-time champions of shareholder value. (A cushion in his office was embroidered with the message, "The one with the biggest cash flow wins."[72]) He knew that to deliver on his commitment, he had to sell a lot of Coca-Cola ("share of throat") and earn healthy margins.

Another executive might have made a meal of this message. Instead, Goizueta homed in on just three imperatives: "acceptability, availability, and affordability." He was wise enough to know that if he got his team to focus on these, they'd figure out what to do.

Follow his logic:

Shareholder value = $ returns
↑
Share of throat = sales growth
↑
Acceptability = quality/branding
Availability = distribution "within an arm's length of desire"
Affordability = prices/costs
↑
Action

Under Goizueta's inspired leadership, the three "A's" got massive attention. Coke staff across the world knew where to apply themselves. The results were extraordinary.

If Goizueta had made his financial goal the big one, he'd have rapidly lost the attention of most people in the company. Firstly, they'd have seen it as *his* problem – too far away to understand or affect. Secondly, they wouldn't have known *what to do about it*.

Goizueta understood the difference between causes and effects. He wanted maximum sales at minimal cost, so that's where he focused everyone's attention. By highlighting the *drivers* of value, he made sure the worldwide team worked like crazy on them.

In some firms, in some circumstances, it might make sense to use the usual four issues of the balanced scorecard as a frame for *high-level* strategy. But just about everywhere else, you'd do better to stress different imperatives.[73]

Financial performance is a *result*. It can hinge on many factors, including the acquisition of other firms, vertical integration, a strong export drive, or expanding distribution. You may need to launch new products or encourage new uses of old ones. Or lobby government for protection, subsidies, or support. Or close plants and retrench large numbers of people.

But while the possibilities are unlimited, your capability for dealing with them is not. So you have to apply your resources where they'll make a difference that matters. And you have to make your goals, intentions, and guiding principles easy to understand and support.

Strategic conversation

Effective strategists understand that communication is a major factor in making things go their way. They anguish about the *content* of their plans, and sweat over their *execution*. They know that the gap between ideas and action is a minefield, and that results depend on many people, most of whom have a very limited view of things.

The boss's best decisions can be killed not only inside an organization, but outside too. Employees, customers, competitors, and many other stakeholders can block them. They can also be nullified by economic conditions, new laws, shifts in social or consumer sentiment, or innovative technologies. An awful lot can go wrong.

But strategy is not just a top-down process. It's not just about getting your way. It's also about *learning* and *adapting* and *improving*.

Just as people in the sales team or the R&D lab might have no line of sight to the CEO, so does she have no line of sight to them – or to customers, suppliers, and the many others who might be a source of valuable new insights or suggestions.

Communication needs to be both top-down and bottom-up. It needs to be informative, as well as inspiring and exciting. But quality is more important than quantity. Endless meetings and flurries of reports, memos, and e-mails guarantee that your ratio of value-adding to value-subtracting work will be out of whack.

To earn the right to be called *strategic conversation*, communication must be purposeful, focused, and systematic. It must happen for a reason. It must be managed. And it must have a timetable.

Crafting the message

The worst thing any executive can do in this complex world is make things seem *more* complex. It's a great leadership skill to be able to unpack and decipher things, provide a clear way forward, and spell out the actions that will ensure progress. Then, to communicate your intentions to key audiences.

The best way, in my view, is to create a picture of your aims. I call it a ValuePlan (Figure 3-3). Here's how you do it:

Step 1 – Define your purpose and priorities. To arrive at your purpose, answer these questions:
1. Whom do we serve?
2. What value do we deliver?
3. Why do we matter?
4. What is our ambition?

To decide on your priorities, ask:
1. What few things must we do to take this company into the future on the course of our choice?
2. What must we do first?

Your first pass at this exercise will no doubt end in quite a lot of words. So do some bold pruning. You want the core ideas, not an essay. You can also add some financial metrics.

Step 2 – Apply the "3x" discipline. The intention here is to make things manageable. So:
1. Reduce your list of issues to the *three value drivers* that you absolutely have to do something about to create value;

2. Specify *three goals* under each driver;
3. Decide on the *three actions* you must take to meet each goal.*

Step 3 – Capture your decisions in a ValuePlan. This is a one-page snapshot of your strategy. It helps you communicate your thinking, and reminds people what really counts.

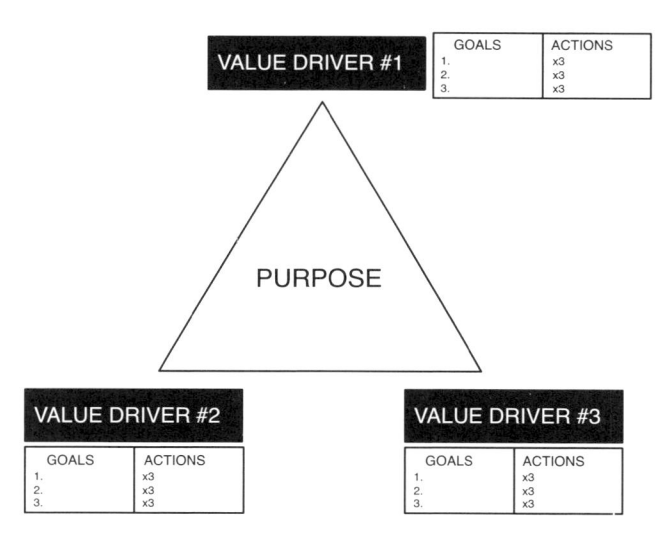

Figure 3-3: *The ValuePlan*

This all sounds straightforward. I've been doing this with companies for several years, and after they've been through it, managers always say, "That was so easy!" But the process is not without pain.

Strategy always demands trade-offs. You can't attack every market, chase every customer, or sell every product. To try is to court failure. You have to make hard choices.

---

* Even following this disciplined approach, you'll wind up with 9 goals and 81 actions. So try to cut the list of actions – or at least ensure that they're shared among a number of people.

But that's precisely why it makes sense to use a triangle as the central element of the ValuePlan. Since it has only three points, it limits the number of value drivers you can include. This forces you to narrow down your list of critical activities.

"But wait a minute," you say. "My business is too complicated to do that. What about using another image, allowing a few more drivers to be included?"

It's a valid question. You might well have to keep a range of issues on your agenda. The problem is, when you cut some slack and allow four drivers, or five, someone will want to add a sixth. When everyone on your team has their say, the list will grow. Before you know it, you'll be right back to square one.

"No" may be the most important word in a strategist's vocabulary. If you don't use it, anything goes and everything is an opportunity.

An effective ValuePlan depends on your saying no to many possibilities. It requires that you say, "This is a priority" … "This can go on the back burner" … or "Forget about it."

By highlighting what you *will do*, it implies what you *won't do*. This keeps your team from constantly returning to issues that are "off the map." It tells other stakeholders exactly what you're about, and therefore what they might expect from you, how they might support you, and so on.

Saying no to business opportunities is not something to do lightly. It deserves careful analysis, thought, and debate. But you must do it.

Simplicity is a powerful competitive weapon. When you reduce your firm's grand intentions to a simple picture, you send an important message. You make sense of difficult issues, and enable people to see the world through clear eyes. At the same time, you provide much needed discipline, and show that you're prepared to make tough calls.

Cascade the energy

The value drivers that sum up your organization's strategy must lead to specific work by people in various parts of the business. You can make this happen by using the ValuePlan framework and thinking process at every level of your organization (Figure 3-4). This makes goals and actions specific to various divisions, departments, functions, and even individuals; ensures that tasks are assigned where they belong; and gives the right people responsibility for the right things.

When individuals throughout your organization can create personal ValuePlans for themselves, you know you're making progress. If anyone can't, you know you have a problem.

Even if there's total clarity, however, the job is not done. Value management is not a form-filling exercise. It's a way of *managing*. More specifically, it's a way of shaping your strategic conversation in order to deliver results.

30-day deadlines

When you scope out any task, time is your enemy. Things always take longer than you imagine. But work also expands to fill the time available.

It has become a cliché that change takes time. Some does. A lot doesn't. One way to create excitement and energy in your organization is to shorten your deadlines, to put intense pressure on people to get things done fast, to remove any chance of "wheel spin."

For several years, I've encouraged executives to think in terms of 30-day strategies. That's right – *30 days*. At first, they think this is ridiculous. But when they try it, they find that suddenly they achieve far more than they thought possible.

Clearly, not all projects can be done in this short time. But, equally clearly, all work can be broken down into 30-day chunks. So, even if you're faced with something that will take, say, six months, ask, "What must we do in the next 30 days to get going?" The results will astound you. Every month, you'll register real progress. In no time at all, you'll have major accomplishments under your belt.

Progress is an important factor in success. So is pressure. The 30-day discipline works wonders.

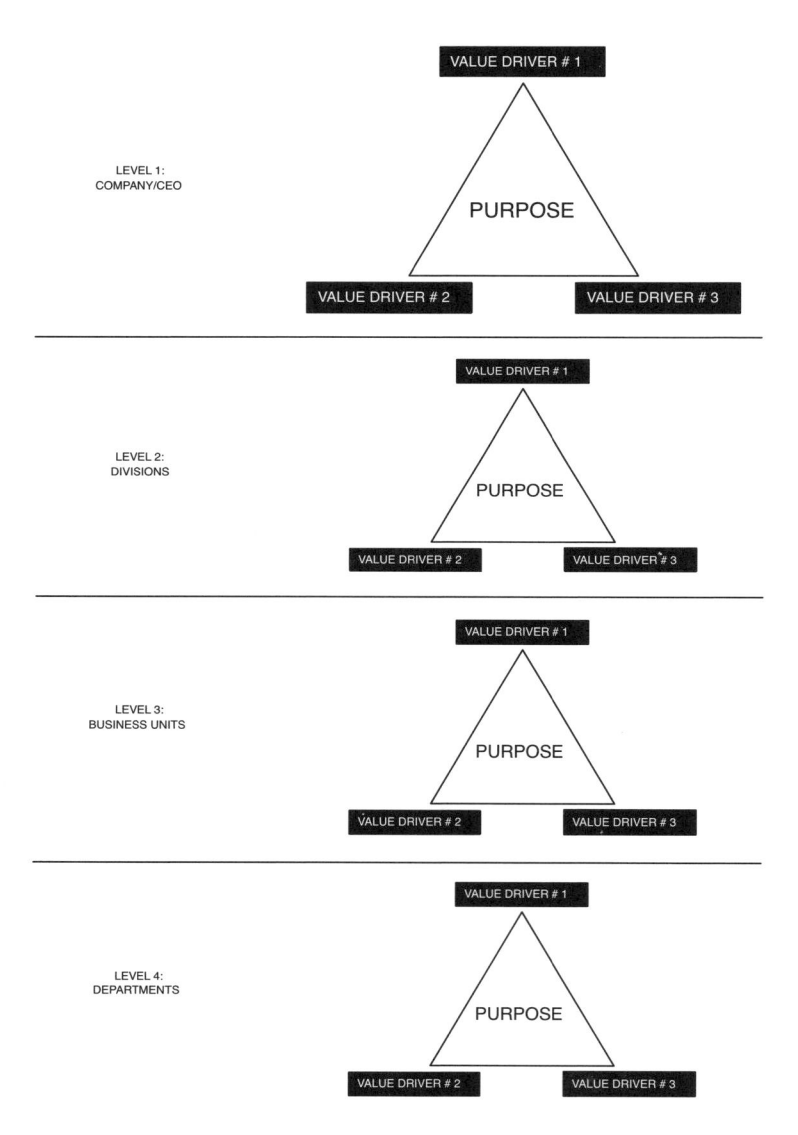

Figure 3-4: *The ValuePlan framework can be used at many levels in an organization*

Definition of a value driver

If a ValuePlan is not the result of rigorous thinking, it's worthless. If it doesn't provide direction and guidance that will make the *right* difference, it's pointless.

As a summary of your strategy, your ValuePlan is a great communications tool. But only if you apply a good deal of discipline when you create it.

Managers are notoriously sloppy with language. Their ideas are often poorly thought through. They assume they're being clear, when in fact they leave a lot to other people's imagination and interpretation. They're ambiguous when they should be specific.

When you talk value management, one term you have to get straight is "value drivers." It's key to your strategy, but often is used so loosely that it means nothing. For example, to speak of "shareholder value," "increased profit," or "market share" as value drivers gives no hint of what a company has to do. These are intentions, not actions. They may be very important ambitions, but the question is: how do you get there?

By definition, *a value driver is an activity that leads directly to the creation of value*. It's a cause, not an effect. Shareholder value, profit growth, and market share are *results*.

Three questions that shareholders ask lead to another three questions that managers must answer:

Shareholder perspective	Management perspective
1. How sustainable is this firm's competitive edge?	1. What must we do to keep our edge?
2. How fast are profits growing – and what is the outlook?	2. What must we do to keep profits growing?
3. Is enough money being reinvested for the future?	3. Where must we reinvest for the future, and how much?

In case you have any doubt about what might or might not be a value driver, here's a test:

1. Is this an *activity* rather than a goal?
2. Do we absolutely have to focus on it to achieve our purpose?
3. Will doing it give us an "80/20" impact?

If the answer to all three questions is yes, you know you're on track. When you put issues through this filter, many fall off the list. Being specific here will ensure that you and your team do the right things – and just a *few* things.

Your ValuePlan must fit

All too often, executives have grand notions of where they want to take their firms, but fail because the company, its strategy, and its action plan are out of kilter.

Every firm faces unique challenges, and itself has unique ambitions, assets, and capabilities. The strategy that works for one won't work equally well for another. It's senseless trying to slavishly copy other organizations with different strengths, facing different realities, and doing quite different things for reasons you may not understand. You have to create the strategy and design the business model that are best for you.

Value management is more than just a matter of decisions. It's also about managing your business in the way that is most appropriate and feels most comfortable. So your action plan must ensure that you do what's right for *you*, not what might be right for someone else. And your whole management approach must be consistent with what you're trying to do.

The purpose of your ValuePlan is to explain your strategy in an easy-to-grasp, graphic way, and to make clear your priorities. It must sit comfortably with your company's strategy and characteristics – its culture, character, history, assets, capabilities, and so on.

4
WHAT GETS MEASURED …

"To collaborate around shared information you first have to develop a shared framework for interpretation."

John Seely Brown and Paul Duguid, *The Social Life of Information*, 2000[74]

Companies operate in a complex world and get banged about by many forces. To say you have to watch your back is no joke. The trouble is, you also have to look ahead and to the sides, and up and down. You can never be sure where the next missile will come from. Nor can you know for sure where tomorrow's opportunities will emerge.

When you look into the future, there are more uncertainties than certainties. The further out you gaze, the fuzzier the view. Laying a bet on a particular outcome is a very dicey business.

Managers like to think they're always objective about this. They pretend to base their decisions on facts and they talk of "managing by the numbers." With the encouragement of investors, journalists, consultants, and academics, they fool themselves that they can sum up the past, present, and future in numbers alone. (Some think that's possible with just one number!)

Almost every popular business magazine and newspaper runs regular scorecards of corporate performance. Mostly, these list readily available data such as sales, profits, assets, and market value. *Fortune* also ranks "wealth creators and destroyers" on the basis of EVA and MVA* performance.

Then there's any number of contests and honours for just about everything from "most admired company" to "best company to work for," from export

---

* Market value-added.

achievement to the famous Baldrige Quality Award. They're all coveted, and companies go to great lengths to win them.

All this hype is exciting for insiders and interesting for outsiders, but not very useful to anyone. The best it can do is reflect what happened in the *past*. But doing well in one year is no indicator of what's to follow. Even a historical trend is of limited value. What's more, firms that rank at the top of these lists in one year often take a dive in the next.

The search for ideal management metrics will never end. There are big incentives for anyone who can come up with something meaningful. But the effort is futile for several reasons:

1. **Many factors impact on share prices.** The "mind of the market" works in mysterious ways. We think great customer service leads to sales and profits – which pleases investors. We think they'll be impressed by our quality, brands, or "human capital." We think that growth in ROI or EVA will do the trick. Common sense says this must all be true, but experience and many research studies say it might not be.[75] In any event, even if you get these things right, other factors might get in the way.
2. **The causes of performance in one firm won't produce equal results elsewhere.** There's no question that the lessons from *In Search of Excellence* were sound. Or that business schools teach valuable stuff. Or that a lot of management journals are worth reading. But companies are all different, and they each have their own challenges. What works for one may not be the answer for another. What one can do may prove impossible for another.
3. **Companies are "prisoners of their context."** Every industry has its own "rules of the game." You might be able to change some of them to your advantage, but there are limits. A fast food business needs one kind of success recipe; a steel maker needs another. The macro environment also dictates to a great extent what you can and cannot do. And the strategies and capabilities that make your firm a winner in one period can cause its failure later, when circumstances change.
4. **Every metric has its weaknesses, and can lead to bad decisions.** There are good arguments for all of them – and good arguments for being damned

careful about them.[76] You can't do without them, but it's what you do *with* them that counts.

There are many ways to *gauge* executive and corporate performance. None is perfect. No single piece of information explains everything. Every measure has its own purpose. All are open to interpretation, manipulation, and misuse. Taken out of context or used in isolation, all of them will tell you useless things and possibly lead you astray.

There are also many ways for executives to *explain* their performance. You need to make the most of them to win the votes of your stakeholders. You should leave no stone unturned in explaining your logic, and doing so in as clear and simple a way as you can.

Failure to tell your story so it makes sense will cost you dearly. It'll impact on your company's share price, its reputation, and its worth. It will also affect your own standing, your ability to manage, and your career.

Needed: a holistic view

Taken alone, any business measure gives you only a partial – and probably quite inaccurate – picture of things. So it's essential that you take an all-round view and try to monitor all the factors that might impact on your performance.

Some of these may be captured in numbers. Some cannot. To pretend otherwise – and to manage only on the basis of limited "hard data" – is unwise. Just as a doctor uses a range of tests to check your health, so do you need a range of "probes" to understand a business.

Because shareholder value is the ultimate issue for business, financial metrics are the ultimate measures of management performance. Financial goals may be needed in many places in your organization. But *financial performance is a result of many activities*. Some of those – not all – need goals, appropriate metrics, and a tracking process.

Control freaks try to measure everything. This is a sure way to draw attention away from the most important things. So where should you start ... and where should you draw the line?

Like it or not, *you have to make assumptions about cause and effect linkages*. Which actions will lead to what results? You might be guided by past experience or the findings of researchers. But sometimes you have to just experiment. Only by trial and error can you really narrow down the possibilities and find what works for you.

The drivers you put on your ValuePlan are the obvious place to start with measurement. As you set your goals for each of them, consider how you'll know if you've been successful. Ask, "What will tell us we've got this right?" Then, as you move forward, keep reviewing your goals – and moving your goalposts.

In addition to financial goals, others to consider include these:
- People – recruiting, diversity, training and development, satisfaction, retention;
- Sales – prospecting, calls, deals, repeat sales, extras (i.e., design, support, financing, warranties, insurance, recycling, disposal, etc.);
- Service and support – customers trained, customer satisfaction, complaints, speed of response, lead generation;
- Manufacturing – inventory levels, cycle times, plant uptime and downtime, maintenance costs, change-over times, productivity;
- Quality – customer satisfaction, supplier inputs, scrap, rework, rejection, waste;
- Innovation – patents registered, new products/services as a proportion of total sales, launch rates, concept-to-cash time, royalties earned;
- Safety, health, and environment – accidents, absenteeism, incidence of HIV/AIDS, spills, clean-up costs;
- Social – investment, communication.

Some of these indicators are *objective*: precise data can be captured, analysed, and reported. Some are highly *subjective*: they're based on opinion, feelings, and attitudes.

Some, such as market share and customer satisfaction, come from *outside* the firm. Others, including sales, quality, waste, reject rates, productivity, and employee satisfaction, are *internal*.

Some show *how* your company is doing in the marketplace ("Here's where we are"), while others help explain *why* it gets those results ("This is what got us here"). And the way you interpret both types can suggest future strategy ("Here's what we must do next").

Obviously, different measures mean different things to different people. For example, financial data might be very useful to the chairman or CEO of a firm, but mean less – or maybe *nothing* – to people elsewhere in the organization. Tracking quality may be critical in the factory but not as important in the HR department. Customer satisfaction measures may help people in sales and logistics, but not in the machine shop. To have real worth, specific measures of quality or service probably need to be different in different places.

You'll be tempted to measure many things. But the discipline of your ValuePlan will help you limit your goals and actions to the few that you'll be able to manage, and that will make the most difference.

Non-financial metrics may be as little use as financial ones in predicting – and thus *managing* – future financial performance.[77] But their popularity is growing, and there's a real risk that firms will adopt too many of them, and wind up unable to cope with the load.

One question that always arises is: *whose targets should you go for?* Should you pick your own or should you benchmark yourself against other firms?

That's up to you. Benchmarking can be valuable, in that it pits you against your peer group, or against firms that perform especially well on specific tasks. But it doesn't work equally well for everything.

Because financials can be calculated and interpreted in so many different ways, it can be hard to compare apples with apples. So your own numbers – arrived at arbitrarily or on the basis of past performance – might be best. Non-financial benchmarks can be more meaningful.

Managing expectations

Stock market behaviour is driven by expectations. In the short term at least, share prices are affected less by a firm's performance than by *gaps between what investors hope for and what actually happens.* In other words, doing well is not enough. Doing what you promised is everything.

Research by Anita McGahan and Michael Porter shows that "businesses that perform differently from the average in one year are likely to perform differently in the subsequent year."[78] Firms can get away with underperformance for a time – as long as it's *consistent* with expectations. And, of course, positive changes are good news.

But a sudden dip sets off alarm bells. Nasty surprises are the kiss of death. As an article in the *McKinsey Quarterly* warns, "a bad quarter, or even a quarter less good than analysts expect, is a bit like a rat on a ship: when you find one, you assume it has company."[79]

In the US especially, executives go to great lengths to meet expectations of their firms' quarterly earnings – expectations that they themselves help to create. According to one study, far more reports meet analysts' expectations exactly or beat them by a penny than *miss* by a penny.[80]

This doesn't happen by chance. "Managing the earnings" is a widespread practice of deceit that benefits no one. Recently, numerous companies including Coca-Cola, PepsiCo, McDonald's, the Washington Post Co., and Gillette have followed the example of Warren Buffett's Berkshire Hathaway* in refusing to give earnings guidance. More are sure to do the same.

Savvy investors are alert to any force that might throw a firm off course. (Just watch the Dow Jones Industrial Index on CNBC or Bloomberg Television on a heavy news day!) They constantly ask, "What's happening out there?" "What does it mean?" "How has it changed my risks?" "What opportunities does it hint at?" "What other changes is it likely to trigger?" "How does it impact on my investment?" (Figure 4-1). Paradoxically, says Lawrence Booth, professor of finance at Toronto's Rotman School of Management, "it is the fact that the market values operations very far into the future, that causes it to react violently to short term results."[81]

---

* Buffett serves on the boards of Coca-Cola and the Washington Post Co., and was until recently a director of Gillette.

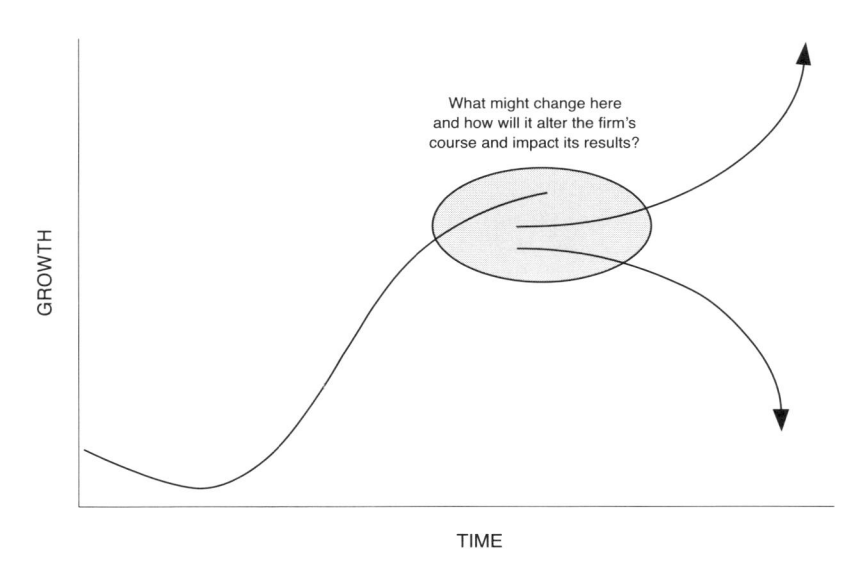

Figure 4-1: *Managers and investors must watch for signs of change*

Executives have to ask the same questions. And they have to provide convincing answers – based on facts, clearly thought through, logical, and mutually consistent. Guesswork is not a good idea. Telling a story that's clear, compelling, and believable is what this is all about.

Beyond the numbers

Investors are less interested in what *has* happened than in what *might* happen. They watch stock prices for the performance they imply. But they also watch a range of other factors that may hint at *changes* in performance.[82] These fall under four headings:
1. **The macro environment** – the impact of politics, economics, society, technology, competitors, and customers on the company;
2. **Industry dynamics** – maturity, structure, key players, new entrants, practices, regulations, etc.;

3. **Stakeholder dynamics** – the current and potential agendas, behaviour, and power of all players who vote for or against the company's success;
4. **Company strategy, culture, assets, and capabilities** – where it is in its life cycle, its market positioning, value proposition, management, skills, technology, brands, patents, reputation, corporate governance, and future intentions (Figure 4-2).

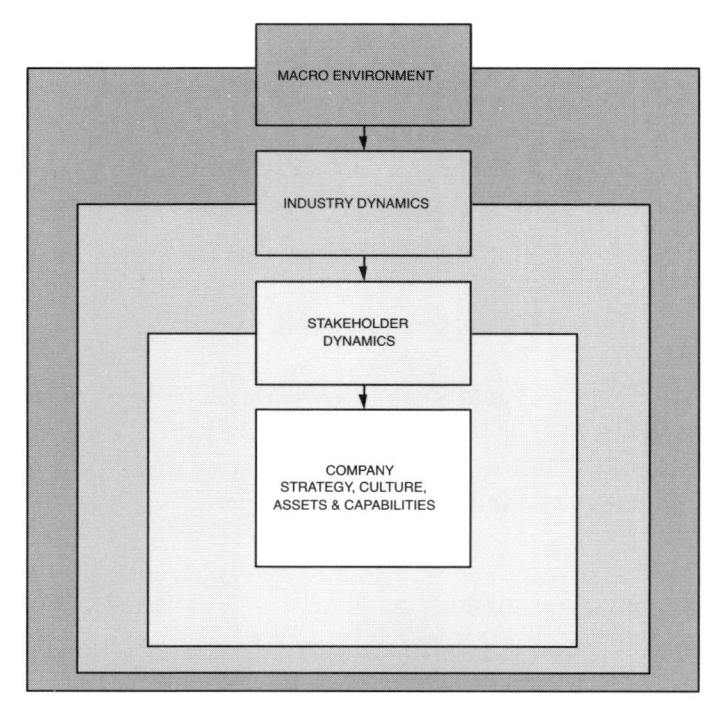

Figure 4-2: *Many factors contribute to an organization's performance – and its share price*

In short, investors want to know:
- What might change in the *outside arena* that will affect this company's fortunes?
- What's happening in this firm's *industry* that might impact on its profitability?

- What might *stakeholders* do that will affect the firm's ability to perform?
- What is *management* doing that will make it more or less competitive in the future?

Having developed a view of the firm's potential from the only evidence they have – its *past* results – they must now speculate on the future. Which way will things go?

Managers clearly cannot control everything that affects the destiny of their companies. Studies show that over a one- to three-year period, *market* and *industry* factors may account for up to 40 per cent of total returns to shareholders (TRS).[83] Yet some firms in every industry consistently do better than their peers. Some are able to shine through good times and bad.[84] This underscores the fact that while managers may have little influence over their share price, they do have a great deal to do with their operating results.

So, while investors monitor the outside environment carefully, they're also acutely aware of management's role. They want to know:
- Can these people do what we expect?
- Are they up to the challenges ahead?
- Is the team being strengthened for the future?
- What is the level of morale in the organization?
- What innovation is taking place?

Increasingly, too, they seek insights about the firm's corporate governance, its ethical values, and its relationships with other stakeholders.

If you leave investors to make up their own minds about what's happening around you and how it'll affect your company, they will. The risk is that they'll come to inaccurate conclusions about both. And they'll punish you if you fail to create the value they expect. So best you look the world in the eye and provide a brutally frank assessment of what you see. Then, be honest about how you're going to deal with it.

You also need to share information with other outside stakeholders such as suppliers, customers, government, trade unions, and the media.

All have their own ways of evaluating your performance. But you can do a lot to shape their views through clear, consistent, and continuous communication. To win their votes you need to give them as complete a picture as possible of what's coming down the line.

So be sure to:
1. Explain your assumptions about the operating environment – "This is what we see happening around us";
2. Identify the value drivers that will make the difference – "This is what we must focus on to produce results";
3. Spell out the actions you intend taking – "This is what we will do, and why it makes sense";
4. Provide regular updates on your progress – "This is how we're doing."

If doing this is vital to the understanding of outsiders, it's even more important inside. Your own people need to know the "why" behind your strategy and your actions, as well as the "what" and the "how." So your strategic conversation needs to work in all directions. The metrics you use to do things differently inside your firm should also help you communicate externally.

The best tools for the job

You can't run your company without numbers. But nor can you run it on numbers alone. If you ignore the "big picture," you'll miss information that might give you the most valuable insights.

Selecting metrics that work for you is critical. The right ones will aid you greatly. The wrong ones will mislead and perplex everyone who deals with them, bog your organization down with unnecessary work, and create dangerous expectations.

Companies are complicated things. There's lots to do. But before you dash out and create a laundry list of things to measure, consider why you need to measure anything at all.

Aside from providing tangible goals and a performance scorecard, appropriate metrics tell you:

- What to keep doing;
- What to improve;
- What to stop doing.

Whatever metrics you settle on, they should:
1. Inspire profitable growth today and tomorrow;
2. Be easy to calculate, easy to understand and use, and easy to track;
3. Help decision-making – about strategy, priorities, actions, and methods;
4. Be meaningful to the people who use them;
5. Encourage your people to work as one team;
6. Facilitate delivery of value to *all* stakeholders.

No matter how hard you try, you'll never hit on the perfect measurement system. There will always be more things to measure than you need to, or have time for. But remember, measurement is only an *aid* to management, not a substitute for it.

When you select your metrics, you should:
1. Balance control with common sense;
2. Opt for simplicity over complexity;
3. Use few measures rather than many;
4. Forget about 100 per cent accuracy;
5. Allow for some subjectivity;
6. Be prepared to change if (a) particular metrics no longer serve you, or (b) others might be better.

Tested against these criteria, many of the approaches currently in vogue are less than satisfactory. In fact, they can be more trouble than they're worth, triggering confusion, friction, and "push back."

When control systems become too rigid or too complex, people fight them. Not even the best measures of value creation lead automatically to the *creation* of value. To know "how we've done" is no guarantee that you'll know what to do next – or that it will be done.

There is a fine balance between having a tight grip on things and strangling performance. Micro-measurement might sound super-smart, but can kill the flexibility that must be the essence of strategy in an uncertain world. Don't try to be so sure about everything that you defy logic and cripple your company by trying to impose systems and methods that fly in the face of reality.

The importance of assumptions

All business decisions are based on *assumptions* ("I think this … so this will happen"). All business measurements, too, are based on assumptions ("We'll use this measurement … because it will tell us this").

Since value management is about the future impact of today's decisions, it depends ultimately on your *assumptions* about the future:

- Will the economy grow?
- Will customers spend more … or less?
- How might competitors behave?
- What might be the impact of new legislation?
- Which way will inflation, interest rates, and currencies go?
- Which way are commodity prices likely to trend?
- Is there a threat of accidents, breakdowns, war, a terror attack, a natural disaster – or some other major disruption – that will suddenly and surprisingly increase risk?

These things are unknowable. The best anyone can do is make informed guesses.

A lot of managers don't think through their assumptions, or test them. In some cases, they're pressed for time. Some are too lazy. But, mostly, they just don't see the need. So it's common even for old hands – or maybe *especially* for them – to rely on vague opinions, dinner table gossip, unfounded rumours, and yesterday's experience. Or to blithely accept "what everybody knows" as being factual, accurate, and a sound basis for decision-making.

To make things worse, they see what they want to see in the world around them – and it's mostly *good*. They look for facts that confirm they're right, rather than evidence that they might be wrong. The bad stuff is filtered out.

According to psychologists, executives tend naturally to be overconfident. Even when events turn against them, they cling to the belief that "things will turn out fine." This leads them, for example, to regularly overestimate their sales targets and underestimate the problems they might face.

As a result of these human failings, plans are created on shaky foundations. Targets are stretched so far as to be ridiculous. Then, in board meetings, senior executives clash with directors who dispute their assumptions. And in discussions with analysts, investors, or the media, they're embarrassed by probing questions and critical comment.

Hopefully, being alert to these traps will save you from them. Being aware you're in the realm of theory rather than fact will keep you from being suckered by a sales pitch, or falling for some "magic number" that's supposed to tell all.

Making your team aware of these pitfalls will sharpen their thinking too. By challenging their views and pressuring them to justify what they say, you encourage both logical argument and clarity in presentations and reports. In effect, you train people to think before they speak, to make a sound case, and to make it well.

The trap of too much information

Although measurement has been an integral part of management practice for the past century, executives keep adding to their load. They use more and more metrics to track a widening array of activities. New technologies put information at their fingertips in real time, and let them slice and dice numbers into ever thinner slivers – supposedly yielding ever sharper insights.

Has all this helped?

Corporate information junkies would no doubt say yes. But their behaviour tells another story.

Firms churn out reports that lie idle on desks. Executives pore over figures, but then fail to act on them. Long meetings are held to make decisions, but the only decision is to set up a task force to get more information, or to plan another meeting.

Watch people at work and it's hard not to conclude that information is their enemy. It either tells them nothing and sends them on a wild goose chase, or tells them a great deal but changes nothing. Huge parts of organizations are dedicated to this industry. It would make a lot more sense to spend more time making and selling stuff. That, after all, is what makes money.

Introducing any measurement approach into a firm is hard work because it means *new* work. First, there's the challenge of understanding the latest tool, teaching people how to use it, and making it part of "the way we do things around here." Then there's the fact that users can quickly be swamped by paperwork, yet be no more certain about what to do next (i.e., "What I must do tomorrow").

At first glance, most metrics look simple enough. In practice, things tend to get complicated. Take, for example, economic profit, a concept that gets a great deal of coverage in business journals, and is the subject of a lot of research and debate.*

Consulting firms that promote it avow that it's easy to understand and easy to figure out. Yet one boasts that its cost of capital calculations may need to be adjusted more than 160 ways. Most say that fine-tuning is needed for different industries. All say it takes time to install their methods in client companies. Heavy commitments to training are essential.

Some firms claim that teaching all their people about economic profit has paid off. But is it really worth the effort? The evidence is mixed, at best.

There might be some benefits in organizations whose staff are mostly knowledge workers, where the structure is simple, and where key numbers are easy to access. Others should probably think twice. To spend time educating people about a theory they won't use, based on numbers they must assume, to arrive at other numbers they can't influence, is a waste of time. There are quicker, simpler ways to get results.

---

* Economic profit = net operating profit after taxes − (capital × cost of capital)

As happens so often in business, a mountain has been made out of the measurement molehill. You can become obsessed about finding the perfect tool, when in fact there's no such thing. And you can go overboard with analysis and number-crunching at the expense of performance.

But why make the job more difficult than it needs to be?

Value management is not brain surgery. Rather, it is just plain common sense – which is probably why it's not common *practice*. To make it work for you, you should probably put your organization on an information diet. Feed it nutritious stuff, but leave out anything that doesn't build muscle, spark the brain cells, and raise its energy level.

5
MONEY MATTERS

"First, there should be an unrelenting focus on making sure that all capital lodged in the business generates returns in excess of the cost of capital ... Second, managers should constantly seek to invest in value-creating projects and strategies."

Michael J. Mauboussin, Credit Suisse First Boston[85]

Value delivery is a result of many activities. *You need various measures to know how you're faring. But a balanced scorecard is not the answer.*

Before you start yelling, let me add another heresy.

The most important measures of business performance are financial. But *it doesn't really matter which you choose as your "lead" measure. Literally any of them will do.*

Ridiculous, you say. Both statements are absolute nonsense! After all, isn't the balanced scorecard one of today's most popular management tools? Aren't big companies in many countries using it, or planning to? And how can anyone argue that just *any* financial measure ranks up there with, say, EVA or CFROI?

Balanced scorecards are gaining in popularity. A lot of companies have them. But, all too often, managers struggle to use them and soon move on to something else that (a) is simpler and (b) makes trade-offs clear.[86]

Explaining the balanced scorecard has itself become an industry. This can only mean there's a big market of perplexed executives out there. And it's the same with metrics: there's a yawning gap between promise and reality, between high-flown theory and on-the-ground implementation.

Companies hope the latest financial metrics will give them definitive answers, but often battle to use them. Or they find that their new measures do little to resolve old problems. They still have to exercise judgement. They still have to make compromises. They still have to watch for deceptive practices. So they quickly return to more familiar ground.

Value management is impossible without hard choices. It's equally impossible if you become a measurement maniac, and forget what really leads to superior performance.

Unlike a balanced scorecard, a ValuePlan doesn't force you to shoehorn must-do activities into a preconceived framework. Instead of dictating what you must measure, it lets you decide for yourself.

Now, we need to find the financial measures that will work best for you.

No certainty

Finance and accounting are critical functions in business. Yet many of the concepts in both areas are extremely long in the tooth. Much of the newfangled stuff isn't of much help. Companies still fail, analysts still make awful calls, and investors burn themselves.

In theory, money metrics serve three main purposes:
1. They help managers manage;
2. They provide guidance for management compensation;
3. They help investors to value firms.

In practice, most measures fall short on every count. Used wrongly, they may induce executives to do foolish things. They can be exploited to justify incentive plans that make no sense. And they may dupe investors.

Ideally, managers should know, "If we do X, the impact on our stock price will be Y." Alert investors could then say, "They're doing X, so the impact on the value of my shares will be Y." But that's not quite the way things work.

The link between management actions, financial metrics, and stock prices is dodgy, to say the least. Investor decisions often appear puzzling.

Sophisticated new measures may be no more informative than those labelled as "old school." They might suggest *direction* – that stock prices are likely to rise or fall – but they do so with little *precision*.[87]

You have to be very brave or very foolish to rely on any one of them when you make business decisions or place your bets. Nor will any amount of fine-tuning or fiddling give you the certainty you want, or eliminate all risk. The measure has not been invented – and never will be – that will give you perfect foresight.

Obviously, if there were "one best way," everyone would latch on to it – and that hasn't happened:

- Despite the efforts of corporate finance experts "to find a rigorous method of pricing equity," says *The Economist*, "such attempts seem to have failed, or there would have been no bubble."[88]
- Kenneth Ferris and Barbara Pécherot Petitt, the authors of *Valuation: Avoiding the Winner's Curse*, note that "the proliferation of alternative valuation frameworks reflects in part the financial community's inability to agree on exactly which factors are the primary drivers of share prices – revenues, accounting earnings, book value, economic income, or discounted cash flows."[89]

As you might expect, however, companies that use "branded" value management approaches are likely to swear by them. (If nothing else, the credibility and egos of senior people are at stake if they confess that they're using a process that doesn't work.)

But the record is spotty and the jury is still out. Only one thing is clear: when it comes to guiding managers and their teams, many metrics are about as handy as an ashtray on a motorbike. They look spiffy, but don't serve the purpose they were intended for. People waste time polishing them, but then don't use them. In some cases, they don't know how. Mostly, there's just no point in trying because it's too damned difficult, it changes nothing, and there's no feedback.

The trouble with accounting

The cliché, "accounting is the language of business," is only partly true. For one thing, *accounting conventions vary from country to country*. There are numerous governing bodies. Generally accepted accounting practices (GAAP) differ, as does company law. While there's some convergence, there remain plenty of gaps.

Then there's the fact that *accounting conversations vary from company to company*. Although firms generally stick to the rules in their reporting – not least because their auditors insist that they do – they tend to use the accounting measures and language that they like best. What one considers "conservative," another sees as aggressive. Each management team has its own way of computing things.

To rely too much on accounting numbers is as silly as watching only one dial on the dashboard in your car, and as dangerous as keeping your eyes on the rear-view mirror while you hurtle through traffic.

There are many reasons why they must be treated with caution. Among them:

- They don't include an opportunity cost of capital;
- They don't factor in the time value of money;
- They're a record of *past* performance, so may not offer any insights into the future;
- They can be easily manipulated and used in a misleading way;
- No single number tells the whole story – taken in isolation, any of them can provide quite the wrong picture of a business's health and prospects;
- A number that indicates excellent performance for a company with a heavy investment in assets might signal mediocrity in another that's "asset lite";
- They may lead to decisions that are good for one part of a company, but bad for the business as a whole.

Of great concern in the information age is the difficulty of accounting for "knowledge assets." Money spent today on research and development, brands, training, reputation building, and the like may not pay off for years. How do you put a value to management capability, specialist skills, locked-in customers, or important relationships?[90]

Baruch Lev, professor of finance at the Stern School of Business, warns that "We are using a 500-year-old system to make decisions in a complex business environment in which the essential assets that create value have fundamentally changed."[91]

Attempts are being made to deal with this issue, but so far with little success. But even assuming someone does find an answer, the fundamental weaknesses in accounting will remain.

Another issue of these times is the "demassification" of business – the shift from "atoms to bits," from "brawn to brain." Information gurus have spread the gospel that assets are a drag on profits. This, together with injudicious use of accounting measures, may lead managers into making bad decisions.

While *every* firm should obviously strive to operate with the lowest possible investment in assets, the reality is that some companies need "stuff." Paper and steel makers can't operate without mills. Car companies need assembly facilities, computerized lathes and presses, and robots. Computer chip makers need costly "fabs."* Retailers need floor space and stock.

In theory, it makes sense to focus on "high value-added knowledge work" such as research, design, branding, and customer service, and to leave the heavy lifting to someone else. In practice, that may be easier said than done.

Some work *can* be eliminated. Some can be outsourced. Some can be done in new ways. But there's a limit to these things. "Make or buy" debates will never end. Somewhere in a value chain, someone has to do the "grunt" work.

What's more, even if processes can be redesigned, actual changes can't be made overnight. In the real world, firms don't just turn off the lights one day and open for business with a skinny new business model the next.

Under pressure, managers are prone to confusing value management with cost-cutting. They put the accent on saving money rather than doing what's good for growth. By taking actions that might help short-term results, they wind up hurting their long-term performance.[92]

Only by keeping your business purpose in mind at all times will you avoid this mistake. Only by staying focused on your strategy will you keep things in perspective and make sound choices. And only by staying "on

---

* Fabrication plants.

message" about your aims will you be able to counter arguments to do the wrong things.

It may well be necessary to emphasize growth in some parts of your firm – at the upper levels, for example, or in the sales department – while people lower down need to concentrate on cutting costs. If so, make sure that *every effort contributes to your growth plan*, and that everyone understands the logic of your actions.

In most companies, executives learn early how to "massage the numbers." They become skilled at "tucking away" a bit here and a bit there for a rainy day, hiding many of their sins, and making poor results look reasonably good. Thus, the picture they show to their head office or shareholders is often distorted. Yet even *they* become captive to its charms. And even if new laws make it riskier for executives to play games, many will continue to do so because it works for them. Flawed reward systems will ensure this.

Add to all this the fact that management information systems may spew out inaccurate data, or produce it too late, and you have a recipe for trouble.

Managers who depend on periodic accounting reports are, in effect, trying to understand a forthcoming movie by looking at a few old snapshots. Looking backwards, they're likely to pay too little attention to the value drivers of tomorrow. And they may fail to see that the numbers they favoured for some reason in the past no longer give them the information they need.[93]

Accounting numbers are most useful when they're seen as trends. They must also always be viewed in the context of what's happening in and around an organization altogether.

It's one thing for returns to slump when the economy is booming, and something else for them to fall when GDP growth slows. Ratios that are acceptable when you're in rapid expansion mode may be cause for worry when you hit white water.

All in all, the "discipline" of accounting is a witches' brew. But accounting measures aren't about to go away. In the pages that follow, we'll look at a way to use them to drive value-creating action in your firm. But before we do that, we need to touch briefly on two concepts – cash flow and the cost of capital – that are central to the process.

You can only count (on) cash

Investors make money in two ways:
1. The value of their shares increases;
2. They get a stream of dividends (Figure 5-1).

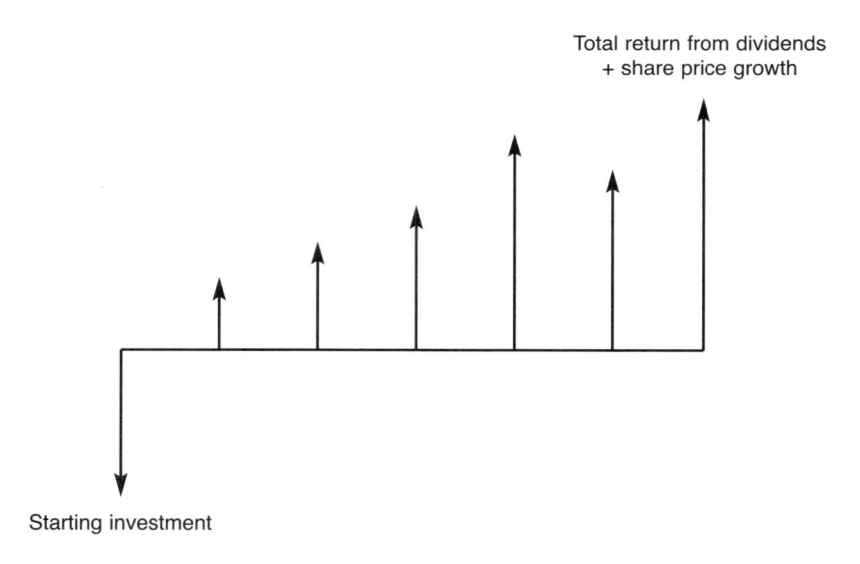

Figure 5-1: *Shareholders aim for share price growth plus dividend flow*

When they evaluate a firm as an investment prospect, they first seek a sense of how much they'll be able to take out of it over its remaining life. Then they discount that number to the present, because a dollar (or rand, pound, euro, yen, or whatever) in the hand is worth more than one sometime in the future.

Obviously, every investment has an "opportunity cost." Cash invested in one firm can't be invested elsewhere. This means that *investors have to make trade-offs*. They have to weigh any perceived opportunity against the perceived cost of taking it. Their test is, "Where will I do best?"

Not surprisingly, they've latched on to the idea that "profit is an opinion, cash is a fact." They know that just because a business shows profits doesn't mean it's in good shape. Companies that "throw off cash" are far more attractive than those that consume it.

Michael Mauboussin of Credit Suisse First Boston likens investment to operating an old-fashioned steam train. The question, he says, is, "How much coal has to be shoveled into the engine to drive the future of earnings in the business?"[94]

Obviously, investors like firms that need little money to produce lots of it. Cash flow tells them a vital story:

1. It indicates whether a firm is able to pay its way, and thus stay in business;
2. It indicates whether they'll get the returns they want.

Because of all this, it's widely agreed that the best gauge of a firm's value is its discounted cash flow (DCF).[95] So when experts buy or sell a company, says Peter Fisher, Under Secretary of the US Treasury, they hire an analyst who "discounts to present value all of the firm's contractually-obligated future cash out-flows … and cash in-flows …"[96]

Ace investor Warren Buffett refers to the resulting number as a firm's "intrinsic" value, and says such analysis "offers the only logical approach to evaluating the relative attractiveness of investments and businesses." But, he warns, getting to a number isn't easy. At best you'll wind up with an *estimate* – and one "that must be changed if interest rates move or forecasts of future cash flows are revised."[97] What's more, two people looking at the same information are likely to arrive at different answers.

Past cash flow isn't in doubt; it happened and you have the facts. Future cash *outflows* can be estimated with some confidence. But there's a huge question mark over *inflows*.

The reason: earnings depend on sales, and forecasting sales is chancy, at best. The system hasn't been invented that will give you certainty. The best you can do as you peer into the future is to make an educated guess about how you'll perform.

Cash flow is no more a panacea for all your measurement problems than is anything else. It goes without saying that there are various definitions and more than one way to calculate it.[98] Long-term forecasts are inherently risky. Short-term cash flow doesn't tell you very much, and managers can easily "tweak" it to suit their agendas.

For all that, though, cash flow generally provides the most truthful view of things. You should pay careful attention to it – and ensure that your people do, too.

The cost of capital

It's pointless talking cash without also considering how much capital you need to create it. If you're not earning *more than the cost of capital*, you're in trouble. The experts might not agree on much else when it comes to measuring performance, but at least they agree on this. Listen to three of them:

- "Until a business returns a profit that is greater than its cost of capital it operates at a loss."[99] *Peter Drucker*.
- "It's not how fast your revenue grows or how big you get. Success – and economic value – can only fundamentally be measured in terms of your ability to earn a sustained, superior return on capital."[100] *Michael Porter*.
- "Shareholder value may be measured as the excess return to shareholders – the amount by which the total return they earn, taking dividends and capital gains together, exceeds the cost of capital."[101] *John Kay*.

So here's the challenge. Companies must ensure that:

Total returns > total costs (including cost of capital)*

---

* Here's how to get a usable figure for your cost of capital:
  1. Estimate how much fixed and working capital you require.
  2. Establish a cost for that capital (both debt and equity). For the debt cost, use the prevailing real interest rate. For the equity cost, check the five-year returns of top-performing firms in both the same industry and a range of industries. (Business magazines list them.)
  3. Decide on a risk factor (what finance professionals call a "beta"). Use the current return on government bonds to know what you could get "risk-free." Then adjust the number to cover the risk you perceive for your business venture.

Once again, when different management teams do the sums, they're sure to come up with quite different answers. They might crunch the numbers to 21 decimal places, but they have to *begin* with some assumptions – about the future cost of capital, and about possible risks. As with sales, it's wise to spell out those assumptions, both to test the logic of your decisions and to make it clear to others. Whatever you conclude, it's just a starting point. After that, the real world takes over.

From intentions to action

If maximizing cash flow and minimizing your capital needs is the goal, how can you do it?

The first step is obviously to review your strategy, and if necessary, change it. (It's pointless doing the wrong things better!) Next, you need to work on your implementation. And, ironically, there's an accounting tool that will help you.

Most managers cut their teeth on ratios like return on investment (ROI), return on equity (ROE), or return on assets (ROA). For reasons that are often unclear, some firms use variations of these, such as return on net assets (RONA) or return on invested capital (ROIC). These are just a few of several dozen ratios in common use, each revealing a piece of the performance puzzle.

Managers are spoilt for choice. However, the good news is that all these indicators are rooted in double-entry bookkeeping, and made clear in the "Du Pont system" (Figure 5-2).*

The original purpose of this chart was to help control the operations of a vertically integrated company. By the 1950s, it was widely used in management accounting textbooks and MBA courses, and a 1976 study of the *Fortune* 1000 rated it the most popular way to explain divisional performance.[102] But those were the days when firms saw ROI as the best way to signal their earnings objectives.[103] In recent times, both the measure and the Du Pont chart have fallen from favour.

---

* Developed around 1919 by a finance executive at E.I. du Pont de Nemours and Co., a chemical company.

Yet both remain extremely useful.

The chart shows how value is created – and how it can be destroyed. It gives investors an "X-ray" of what's going on inside an organization. It helps business unit managers understand why they get the results they get, and identify levers for change and improvement. And it shows how action taken in one area can impact in another.

Although few finance or accounting textbooks mention this octogenarian framework today, it's due for a comeback. While critics warn that it has weaknesses, the same can be said of just about every financial tool.

None of them is ideal. All have their own quirks and flaws. But only a poor workman blames his tools. The rest just make do and get on with the job at hand.

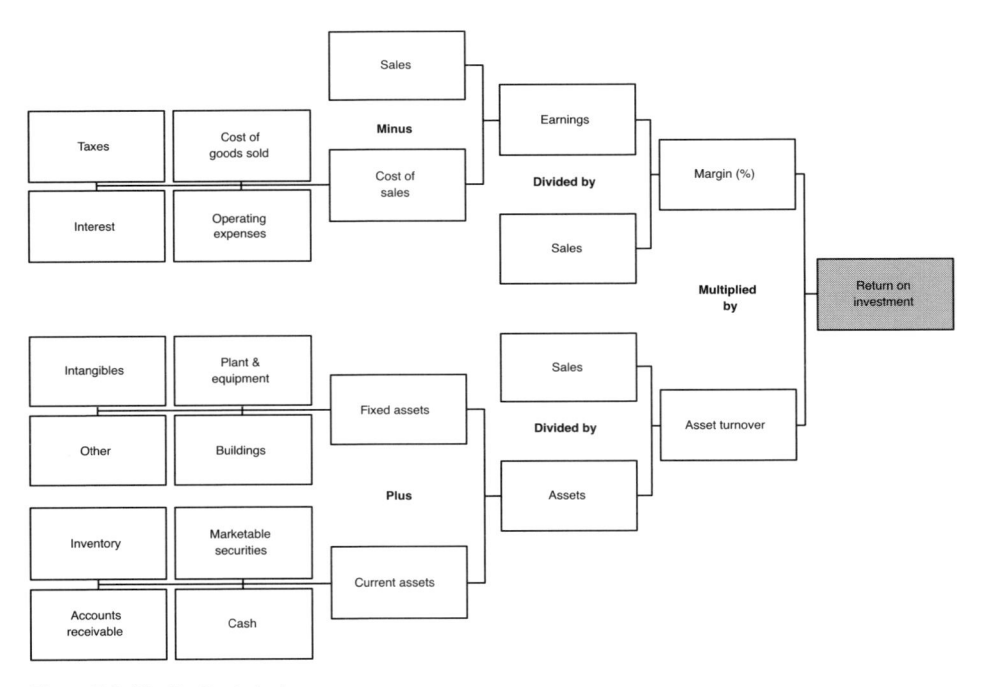

Figure 5-2: *The Du Pont chart*

Choosing your "hill"

The Du Pont chart can be used to calculate ROI, ROE, or ROA. So which should you go with?

This is a debate that could go on forever. But there's no definitive answer. Each of these ratios has its place. All will remain popular, and you need to make up your own mind about which you like best.

Naturally, the biggest fans of any measurement approach are firms that have recently started using it. But *satisfaction* with either a metric or a method doesn't translate into better financial performance.[104]

The experience of many companies suggests that you might as well just flip a coin to pick your key metric, for all the difference it makes. The number itself appears to matter less than the fact that you (a) measure things at all, and (b) talk often about the fact that you do it, and (c) use what it tells you.

But it does make sense to give the options careful thought. Then, to make a decision you feel comfortable with, and that you can justify and explain with conviction. Above all, you should stick with your choice, and avoid the temptation to chop and change. Just as a golfer would probably do best by keeping her old clubs and changing her swing, so would managers benefit by staying with a tool and *managing* differently.

A *single* financial goal at corporate level gives direction, sets the scene for both financial and non-financial goals elsewhere in your firm, and provides a context for all decisions and actions. You need to establish it first, to be able to sensibly decide what else to measure, where, and how.

Start by defining what "success" means to your firm. Then establish an overall performance target. This goes into the centre of your ValuePlan.

For investors and top management, ROI or ROE appear to be the obvious choices. However, you may prefer ROA, since it homes right in on the all-important issue of how you use your assets. (Remember the question: "Do we deliver as much value from the assets entrusted to us as the best performer in the world could do?")* And at an *operational* level, ROA is clearly what you need to work on, as it highlights the actions that matter most.

The point is, you should choose just *one number* as your lead goal.[105] Your purpose is to tell your team, "There's the 'hill' we're aiming at." More than one hill is a recipe for trouble.[106]

Now, consider what you must do to get there – to deliver your intended result. This will suggest other goals, such as earnings growth, margins, or asset turnover.

Before you make your list too long, though, be clear about what you hope to gain. Every number you add makes communication harder and confusion more likely. All the numbers in the world are not going to make you more effective.

Principles before precision

Financial reporting is supposed to be accurate. You should expect your accountant to put "right" numbers on your desk. But don't be too anal about your *goals*.

If you had plenty of time and no pressures, and if you operated in a predictable environment, you might have a case for being spot-on with your maths. But that's not the situation any firm is in. Instead, uncertainty, ambiguity, and volatility are givens. Management is a messy activity that occurs in a messy world. No amount of analysis or complex computation will substitute for judgement, learning, and adaptation.

Little about business is precise. Even the smartest, most qualified people can't get everything 100 per cent right. "Analysis paralysis" is a real and costly threat. Yet the very managers who warn against it keep right on slogging away to ensure it sets in!

With uncertainty all about, it makes little sense to strive for perfection in your calculations. Unless you're plain lucky, the chances of being spot-on are

---

* The average ROA of the top 50 firms on *Fortune*'s list of the 500 largest US corporations in 2003 was just 3,7 per cent. Excluding exceptionally bad performance by AOL Time Warner, the average was still just 5,52 per cent (*Fortune*, 14 April 2003).

slim. So you should be *as strict as you need to be, and no more*. Don't waste time torturing fractions.

Understanding and agreeing on a principle is more important than trying to nail down a future you can't see. Generals know that when the first shot is fired, the battle plan changes. Business leaders need to accept that this applies in their world too. Your sole interest should be in cutting to the chase and getting results.

Working out some key figures will focus your mind and perhaps cause you to see problems or opportunities that you might otherwise miss. But diminishing returns come quickly. Chances are, your first quick-and-dirty calculations won't be far off the mark. More sweat won't give you more useful information.

Your aim should be to provide *guidelines* – not a Holy Grail. It's what you *do* with your goals that matters, not the numbers themselves. So do what will impact meaningfully on the way you *run* your company, and no more.

This advice will fly right in the face of what value management consultancies will tell you. Accountants and economists will howl with indignation at such sloppiness. But remember, some people have a vested interest in selling you a package that needs their input – and preferably for a long time. For them, explaining things in words of one syllable is not a priority.

Of course, for major decisions about where to lay your bets, you should consider various scenarios and test a range of numbers for sales, the cost of capital, risk, and so on. This helps you weigh up your options and their possible outcomes and impact. In most other cases, however, back-of-the-cigarette-box metrics will do.

Training and communication

Life doesn't have to be as difficult as many firms make it. They set off on the wrong foot when they ask, "What's the best way to measure and manage our performance?" The real question should be:

What must we do to deliver superior value?

The issue is not one of *measurement*. Measures are a means to an end, not the end in itself. Only by moving beyond a hunt for the perfect metrics will you get closer to your real goal: making the difference that stakeholders expect.

The real issue is *management*. More specifically, it's *strategy* and *communication*.

First, you have to decide where and how you will compete. Only when you know that can you sensibly decide what to measure. And only *then* can you choose the measures that will be right for the task at hand. This is an ongoing task. As you adapt your organization to new challenges and possibilities, so must you review your metrics, and if necessary change them too.

Second, you have to decide who needs to know what about your strategy, and how you'll inform them. And your strategic conversation must be carefully crafted and conducted, so you deliver your message in the way that works best for you.

In a company of any size, every employee doesn't need to know – indeed, won't be helped by knowing – every detail of the strategy or finances. Besides, it's impossible to make a lot of this information meaningful to them. And even if they did understand it, they wouldn't be able to *do* anything different.

Take a call centre, for example. Is it really feasible that someone whose job is taking telephone orders would have a useful point of view about where to locate the facility and how much to pay for rent, the kind of phone system to install, whether to buy or lease it, or when to invest in a new one? And once the system is in place, what impact might rank and file people have on staffing levels, compensation, and all the other elements of a functioning organization?

Factory workers must make stuff. Salespeople must sell it. The heads of departments have vital operational tasks from which they shouldn't be distracted. To try to make all these people financial experts is a sure way to take their eye off the ball. To burden them with sophisticated calculations of the cost of capital – *over which they have no say and which won't affect what they do* – is pointless.

This is obviously touchy territory. I've consistently advocated maximum involvement, maximum openness, and no-holds-barred communication. But while that's the ideal to aim for, practical pressures usually dictate a less democratic course.

People in different parts of a company need different information. A "one size fits all" approach ensures that no one gets precisely what they require. Just as your leadership style has to be adjusted to the individual before you at a particular moment, so should metrics be tailored to suit them and their jobs.

All of your people should understand three basic tenets of business:
1. Companies must earn more than their cost of capital;
2. Cash is more significant than profit;
3. You must "sweat your assets" to make more money than you use.

Then, they need to know what that means to them. In other words, how they can help cover the costs of capital and generate cash by sweating the assets.

So give them goals, but go light on theory. Give them information they can *use*, rather than a lot of guff they'd sooner forget. Most importantly, make sure everyone knows *why* the measures matter.

Whatever metrics you finally select, it's vital that they match your needs. Don't waste time on snappy acronyms or fancy formulas just for the sake of having them, or because *everyone else* seems to have them. Simplicity and brevity must be your watchwords. To pick just one measure and use it well is far better than having 10 and using them badly.

If you add up all the measures needed across your company, you'll probably wind up with quite a long list. But remember, *you* don't have to do everything. Many issues belong with other people. So be sure that your own list – and every other person's – is short, focused, and specific to each of you.

Du Pont analysis should be a regular feature of your strategy discussions. It provides a powerful framework for educating your team, and for provoking debate about where you need to change your strategy. So we'll return to it in Chapter 6, to use it as an aid to designing and executing your strategy.

But always use it with a clear understanding of its limitations. And always use it in the context of all the other factors that influence business performance.

6
MAKING IT WORK

"... what's critical is to proactively choose what, when, and where to begin so that you have the greatest chance for success in the required time frame."

Jeanie Daniel Duck, *The Change Monster*, 2001[107]

It's time to stop talking and start doing. But where to begin?

When people are asked to "develop some ideas" in a brainstorming session, they flail about. Without a clear framework for their thinking, they don't know how to get going. But given a starting point – a topic, a problem, a challenge – they quickly start throwing out ideas.

Value management isn't a one-time activity. To pay off, it has to be the way things are done every day, in every fibre of the firm. There has to be a mindset that makes value delivery the overarching theme, the obsession, the passion. At the same time, there must be practical ways to deal with the factors that drive or destroy value.

Every company has to *focus* its resources to drive customers' perceptions of *value up*, yet at the same time drive *costs down*.[108] But what does this mean to people in a factory or back office? How can you turn these intentions into action?

Some managers might be able to breathe life into this concept, and help their people think about it and generate valuable ideas. Many will struggle. So here are some ways to shape and guide conversations that will produce relevant answers.

Possibilities ahead

Every company leaves money on the table. Every company does less well than it might at driving value up and costs down. So every company has growth opportunities. Some of them might be hard to see. Many will be right under your nose. You only have to look, and there they are.

Bring back the trusty Du Pont chart, and answers become evident.

It's a brilliant tool for simplifying and focusing conversations and explaining to people where they can make a difference. Every box on the chart offers you an opportunity to change something that will improve your performance. You might want to address all of them at some stage. But there's a way to short-circuit this process for rapid results.

Financial performance ultimately hinges on just two things: *profit margins* and *asset turnover*.[109] Improve those, and your ROA goes up. That's not all you have to do to deliver value to your shareholders, but it's a key task.

Changing these two numbers is less complicated than many people think. There are just four ways to do it (Figure 6-1):

1. Sell more units (of your product or service);
2. Increase prices;
3. Sell faster (increase stock turn);
4. Cut costs.

These actions are basic drivers of financial success. They apply to every firm in every industry. So they must be the fundamental goals of all strategy.

Be specific about where you start

With those four goals in mind, you need to be specific about what you want your people to do next, so they'll tackle the high-impact tasks first. So return to a complete view of the Du Pont chart. Figure 6-2 highlights eight areas where you might get to work. Chances are that many people will have suggestions about these.

Of course, you might see an opportunity to reduce your interest charges or taxes, but these are consequences of the way you operate. So first you have to change some aspect of what's probably been taken for granted for a long time.

As you explore possibilities, be sure that you begin with the ones you can

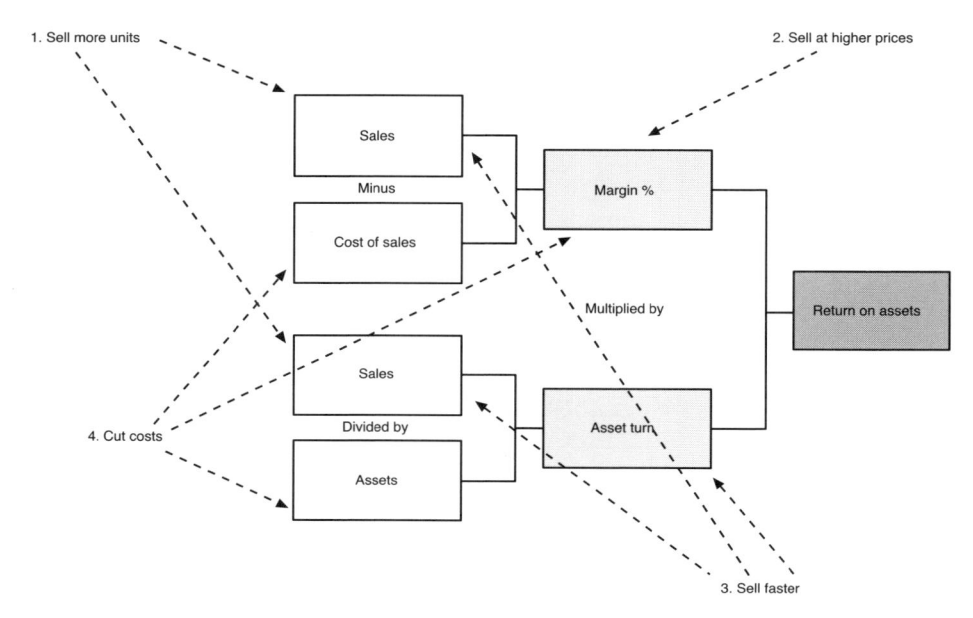

Figure 6-1: *Four ways to improve profits*

do something about right away – the ones that will give the biggest, quickest payback. And consider their potential impact somewhere else. Often you'll be able to kill two birds with one stone.

Imagine, for example, that you decide to go on a sales drive. How would that affect your stock levels? Or your production processes?

Okay, so what about building to order? That would let you cut inventories (of components, work in process, finished goods, or "dead stock"). Then you could streamline your factory and cut the amount of storage space you need. Along the way, you'd cut waiting time in the plant … reduce interest costs … owe less to suppliers … improve maintenance … and so on.

Getting rid of fixed assets such as buildings or plant and equipment might be a vital step. But can you do that today? If you plan to do it in, say, six months' time, what must you change right now to make it feasible? Seeing ways to

106   competing through value management

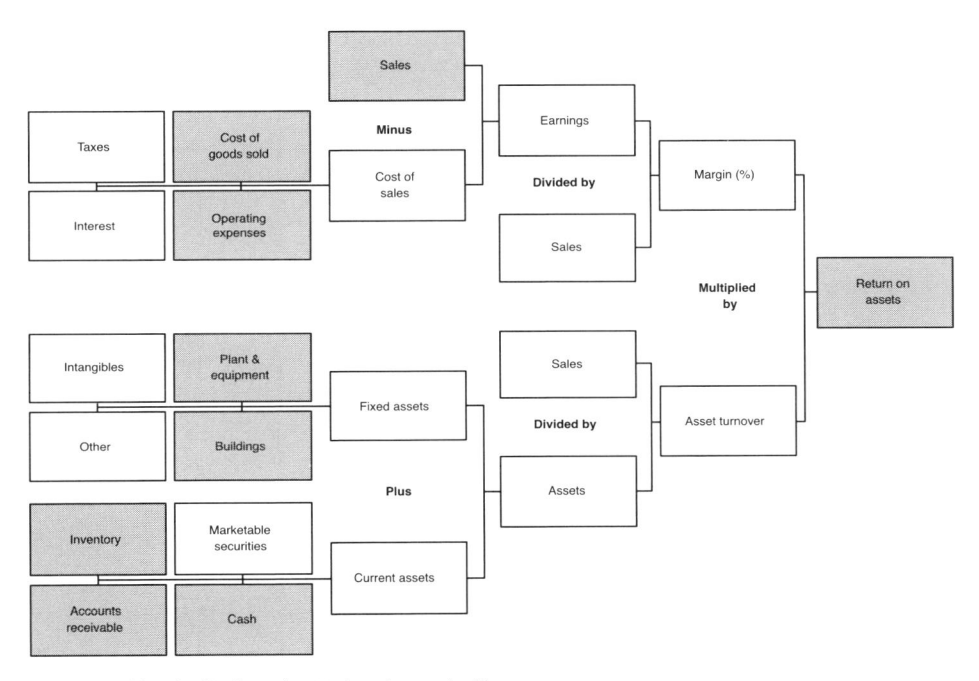

Figure 6-2: *Use the Du Pont chart to target opportunities*

shape up is one thing. You also need to turn those opportunities into work – into projects that people can get their hands around and manage methodically.

First, shed flab

Costs are Target Number One for urgent attention in just about every company. Every cost to your business should be put on trial for its life. If it doesn't add value, and if it won't make you better off in the future, eliminate it.

Don't reduce it.
Don't shift it to another budget.
Don't ignore it.
Kill it!

There are always excuses for not doing this. It'll upset people or cause disruptions. Cuts in one place will cause problems elsewhere. There are more important things to do. And, best of all, "We'll upset our customers."

When times are tough, managers readily haul out their red pencils and attack their costs. It's the logical thing to do. But while cost-cutting may be a vital first step to keeping you in business, it should never be only an emergency tactic.

Costs have to be managed every day, in every part of an organization. Let up for a second, and they come creeping back.

Managers like to think they're tough about this. But they send mixed signals by being tight about minor expenditures, while justifying the need to splurge on conferences or golf days. They also commonly "drag their past into the future."

When you use last year's budget as the basis for next year's, you carry a lot of baggage. Every company has "sunk costs" – money spent on plant and equipment, training, promotions, and much else. Some might be of benefit sometime. Much of it won't make any positive difference. Either way, it's hard to forget. So when managers sit down to plan for a new year, they have yesterday's numbers in their heads. Even though they might grasp the logic of "zero basing" their budgets, few actually do it.

People get remarkably inventive about justifying past decisions and protecting pet projects. It's often difficult to separate what has potential value from what will be a burden. New managers need to be careful about hastily writing off investments made on someone else's watch.

Remember, controlling costs is not a growth strategy. As the saying goes, "You can't cut your way to greatness." The more you cut, the more marginal is the impact of each cut. And sooner or later you'll cut too far, and cripple your business.

That said, getting better results in most firms demands urgent – and radical – cost cuts. This is always painful. People are usually the biggest cost, and reducing headcount offers the quickest way to make a big impact. But if it has to be done, it must be done.

One way to get costs out of the system is to have managers do a line-by-line review of their expense budgets. When you get the first results, send them back for another look. Then another.

You'll certainly save money this way. But seldom as much as you need to – or as much as you might.

So come at the problem from the opposite direction. Pick a number as your target. Challenge your team to meet or beat it.

I often do this with clients. In some cases, I base the number on what I know about them. But sometimes I just pluck a number out of the air – a really *big* number – and throw it at them. No one likes either approach. The second one, particularly, gets plenty of opposition. But then I suggest that we stop arguing and start working on the challenge. And, almost without exception, people take it seriously and very quickly find ways to get the job done.

Effective leadership is about getting people to venture to places they've never dreamed of. Stretch goals can either turn people off or turn them on. Making a serious difference to your costs is a serious leadership test.

Sell! Sell! Sell!

Prudence and conservatism are virtues in business. But an obsession with costs can easily draw attention away from the other side of the value equation, and the lifeblood of every firm – *sales*.

As Figure 6-1 shows, three of the four profit-boosting opportunities involve sales. Only one is about costs. Yet because cutting costs appears to be easier and quicker than increasing sales, costs get priority attention.

As sales slide, savings become more important. So you close a few branches, fire some salespeople, and trim your promotional budget … so sales fall some more … so it's back to your operating expenses with a red pencil. And the downward spiral feeds on itself.

Sales pay for everything. If your companies made enough sales, many of your problems would vanish. If you could predict future sales accurately, you'd be able to do more of the right things and avoid many pitfalls.

There's no way to be sure what you'll sell tomorrow. But you won't come close to knowing if you simply accept what your salespeople tell you. Or if you fail to see the difference between what's *possible* and what's *likely*. Nor is there any process or technology that will give you certainty.

Sales forecasting is a critical matter. Yet too many companies bet the farm on straight-faced promises from salespeople who have no idea *where* the next deal will come from, let alone *how* to close it, or *when* that might happen. Managers accept stupid assurances because doing so gives them hope and keeps the conversation comfortable.

Delivering value demands hard facts, not wishful thinking. If you're serious about making it happen, you have to instil a tough-minded, straight-talking discipline into your organization. People need to know that they can't simply toss empty promises into the ring and get away with it. They need to do their homework, deal in specifics, and tell the truth when they don't know.

Get the best price

You don't have to be a genius to increase sales by giving away your products. But you won't make money that way either. It's imperative that you get the best possible price for every unit you sell.

As we saw in Chapter 1, there's downward pressure on prices in most industries today. But that doesn't mean you should volunteer to discount yourself to death.

If you can't get the prices you want, it's possible you're charging too much. You might have created a "price umbrella" under which your competitors eat your lunch. So check your price/performance offering against theirs. If it's way out of line, you have a problem.

If it isn't – or if some competitors are charging higher prices than yours – you have to look elsewhere. *At your own organization.*

One reason companies start cutting prices is that their own salespeople tell them it's the only way to compete. Under pressure from customers, the road warriors report, "We're too expensive. They won't buy. Our competitors are killing us." When that gets said often enough back at the office, it becomes a fact in the sales manager's mind. She spreads the word. In no time, everybody buys in.

More often than not, the real problem is simply that *your price hasn't been properly explained*. Customers don't understand it. They can't connect your number to their perception of value.

As with so much else in business, getting your price is a communications challenge. Perhaps you need to explain the value in your offering better. Or maybe you need to "unbundle" your price, and show how it's made up.

Whatever your strategy, pricing is an issue that demands a lot of attention. You need to be confident enough to say to customers, "There is no free lunch," and then to explain convincingly to them why they're getting maximum value for their money.

It may be that cutting prices is the smartest thing you can do right now. But it could equally be the dumbest. So before you fall for the moans of your sales staff and give in to pressure from customers, think carefully about the alternatives. Many companies give away profits when there's no good reason to do so.

Opportunity search

There are many places to start looking for new business opportunities. There are countless models, frameworks, and questionnaires that can be of immense help. But, in my experience, most firms need first to think through some fundamental issues. So, before you complicate things, start here:
1. Review your target market/s and your business model;
2. Map the "profit pool";
3. Define your sources of advantage;
4. Fine-tune your value proposition;
5. Attack with a "flurry of blows";
6. Make selling systematic.

All of these are easy to do. You don't need special training. You can involve members of your team in doing this important work right away.

Preparation is essential. You need information to make sensible decisions. Some will be in your database. A lot will be available through desk research. You might also need to get out and talk to customers or suppliers. And you might require help from a market research firm or management consultancy.

Gathering information is a valuable learning experience. You'll gain most from doing as much as possible with your own resources. A first-hand sense of things will generally serve you better than even the most expert outsider's views.

Perfect knowledge is not possible. So even while you collect facts and figures, get to work on these tasks:

1. **Review your target market/s and your business model.** All strategy has to be based on three questions: *Who* is our customer? *What* value will we offer? And *how* will we do it?

   To use your assets wisely, you have to know exactly what you're going to do tomorrow to grow your sales and profits – and to create value. Figure 6-3 outlines your options. You can:
   - Continue selling what you already sell to your current customers (I);
   - Keep doing that, but also chase new customers (II);
   - Stay with the customers you know, but sell them something different (III);
   - Chase new customers with new offerings (IV).

When you decide which customers to aim at, remember that the question is not just "who is our customer?" but "who is our *right* customer?" Which ones do you really want? Who will be best for your company?

Constant thought about *tomorrow's* customers is vital. If you're not one step ahead of your competitors in anticipating where business will come from, you might not have a business.

But while you look ahead, be sure to give your *current* customers their due. Don't neglect them when you search for new opportunities. This happens far too often, but there's no point in chasing after strangers when your database contains a goldmine in unexploited business.

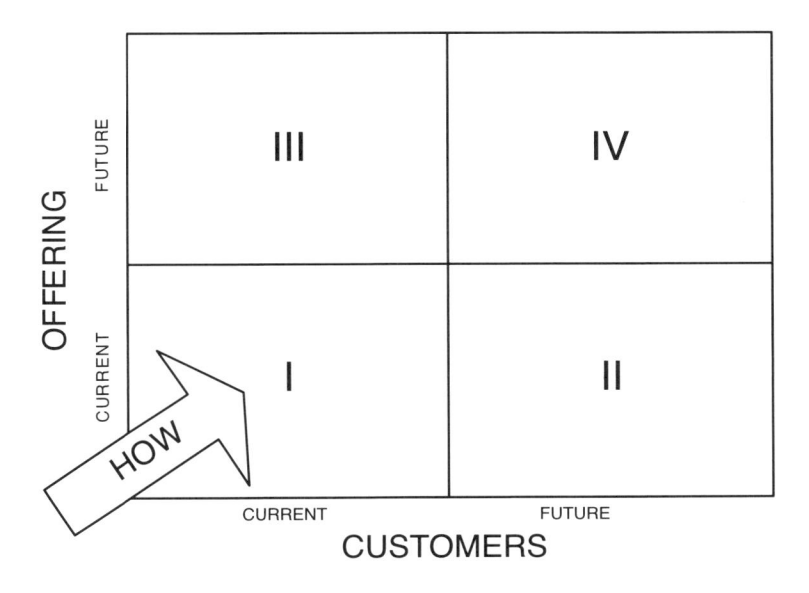

Figure 6-3: *A simple matrix helps you identify opportunities for growth*

Whichever customers you aim for, be sure to consider all possibilities for doing more and better business with them. In addition to selling more units, you should strive to sell "extras" – service, support, finance, guarantees and warranties, parts and accessories. Also, consider the opportunities for testing new products and new sales strategies.

In every case, look for ways to *change how you do things* (your business model), so you sell more, and at a higher profit. It's possible that with only minor changes, you might dramatically improve your results. But radical transformation can't be put off forever.

Sooner or later you have to make fundamental changes to the way you do business. You have to review everything you do, and the way you do everything. Until this happens, you can't be sure you're making the most of your assets.

The framework in Figure 6-4 is an excellent tool for starting an opportunity search. (There's a lengthy questionnaire on my website – www.tonymanning.com – that will help you work through it systematically.)

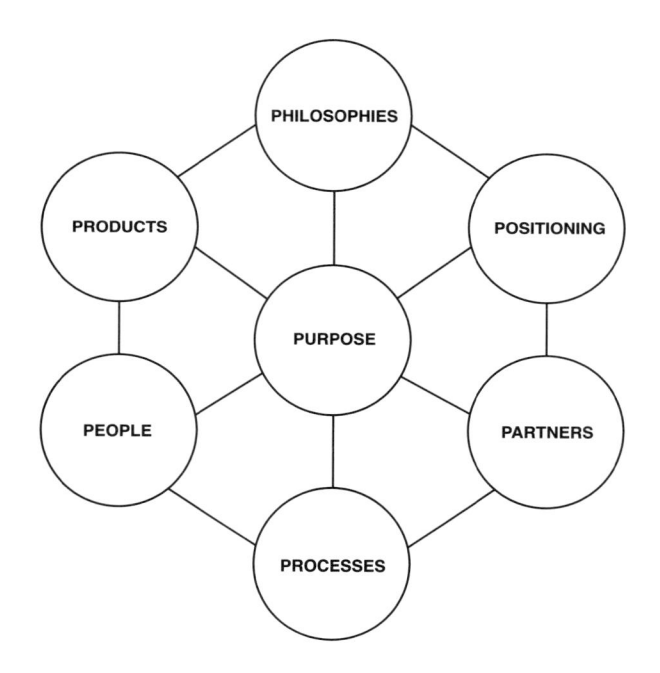

Figure 6-4: *The 7Ps provide a framework for creative thinking about your business model*

2. **Map the "profit pool."** Every business opportunity has its own "profit pool" – the total amount of money available to everyone who adds value. Typically, this pool of cash is divided unevenly. Some players get more of it than others – not always in proportion to the value they deliver (Figure 6-5).[110]

In the past, companies liked the idea of vertical integration, because it gave them maximum control over their businesses. Today, an increasing number of them deliberately unbundle their value chains and outsource bits

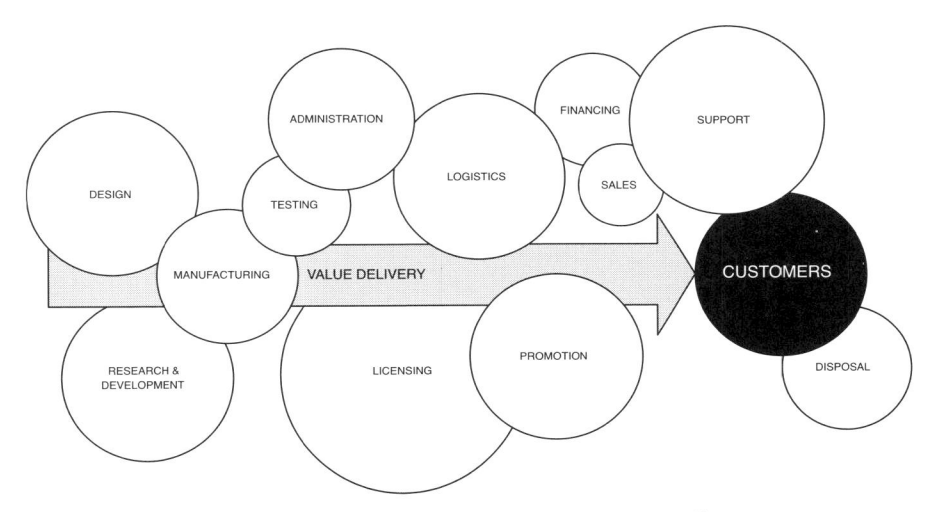

Figure 6-5: *By mapping where profit is created, you can choose your opportunities*

to various suppliers. This lets them focus on their core competences while exploiting the best expertise available for other functions.

Firms don't always do this voluntarily or deliberately. Sometimes, they lose out to competitors who see opportunities to provide a specific input, and seize control of activities that suit them.

By mapping your profit pool, you gain a sense of where there's money to be made, and how much, in the total scheme of things. You'll almost certainly see opportunities you hadn't thought about before. You'll also see potential threats. Thus armed, you can decide on your strategy.

3. **Define your sources of advantage.** How do your customers define "value?" If you don't know, you're sure to offer them "un-value" – features and services they don't expect, don't want, and won't pay for.

Strategy is about connecting a company and its customers. This interface happens in various ways and at various levels. Obviously, the more links you can make, the better. Plug into one need, and you may win a sale and maybe even some repeat business. But connect in multiple ways, and you start to embrace your customer. This makes future sales more likely, and makes it harder for competitors to find gaps.

In a best-selling book of 1995, *The Discipline of Market Leaders*, authors Michael Treacy and Fred Wiersema argue that the best competitors shape their strategies around three "dimensions of value" – product leadership, operational excellence, or customer intimacy. The trick, they say, is to seek absolute leadership in one and to deliver "threshold standards" in the other two.[111]

More recently, in *The Myth of Excellence*, Fred Crawford and Ryan Matthews suggest that every business transaction hinges on *five* factors: price, service, access, experience, and product.[112] Great companies, the argument goes, select one and aim to be best at it.

These are catchy formulas, and they do help ensure that value propositions are clear and focused. But there's a simple flaw in them. What if your "dumb" competitors don't realize they should lead in just one area, and instead push the limits on more ... or even all of them? (Examples: Dell Computer, Toyota Lexus, Amazon.com, Bell Equipment.)[113]

When customers buy almost anything, they weigh up many factors. So while it's important that you make your "unique selling proposition" single-minded and easy to understand, you also need to be sure of hitting all the buyer's hot buttons. Depending on what you're selling, there may be 10 or more of these (Figure 6-6):

a. **Functionality** – How well does the product/service do what's expected of it?
b. **Quality** – How closely does it conform to specifications and satisfy customers' expectations?
c. **Price** – How expensive is it relative to other offerings?
d. **Access** – How easy is it to find/buy/use?
e. **Image** – What is the customer's level of awareness of it, and how favourable is their perception?
f. **Standards** – Does it set or conform to industry standards/is it the benchmark in its category? How important are those standards to customers?

What effect do they have on the actions of competitors and on providers of substitutes?
g. **System** – Is it part of a system that offers complete value? How critical is it for customers to buy into the system?
h. **Service** – How easy/pleasant is it to buy and own this product?
i. **Support** – What systems and structures are in place to ensure future satisfaction?
j. **Experience** – How easy/entertaining/satisfying is the customer's overall purchase/ownership experience?

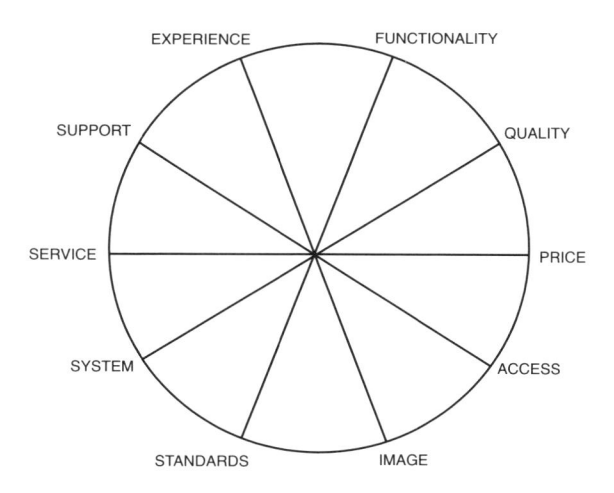

Figure 6-6: *Factors that impact on customer perceptions of "value"*

These factors aren't mutually exclusive. The fact that you rate high on one doesn't mean you can't also do well on the others. You should strive to push the limits on each of the areas that matter to customers.

Once you've ascertained what these are, you can map your offering against those of competitors. This lets you see where you need to maintain your performance, where you need to do more, and also where you might be doing too much (Figure 6-7).

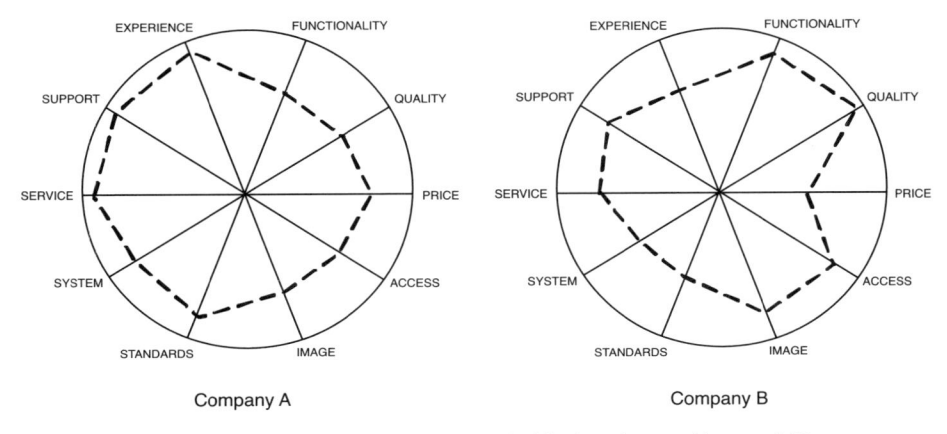

Figure 6-7: *Mapping customer perceptions gives a valuable view of competitive possibilities*

4. **Fine-tune your value proposition.** To make your sales and promotional messages as potent as possible, you have to know what you're trying to say. Many companies don't. Their ads say one thing, their press releases another, and their salespeople something else.

    If you don't know what you want to say about yourself, don't expect customers to work it out. And don't expect them to hear what you want them to hear.

    If you send out mixed messages, one thing is certain: you'll confuse everyone and waste a great deal of money. Whatever "brand-building" you think you're doing will be watered down.

    Crafting an effective value proposition begins with some questions:
    - Who is our "right" customer?
    - What do they buy?
    - How do they buy?
    - When do they buy?
    - How do they define "value?"
    - What value do we offer?
    - What is our "difference?"

- Why do we matter?
- What do we want customers (and others) to know and feel about us?
- How do we want them to respond?

When you've thought this through, one further question remains:
- What must we say to persuade them to do what we expect, and how must we say it (Figure 6-8)?

Your value proposition should come down to just a few words or a few bullet points – "This is why we're the best business partner for you…." Any more than that, and you'll have problems getting it across. You'll also cause difficulties within your organization, both when you try to make your business model relevant, and when you try to execute your strategy.

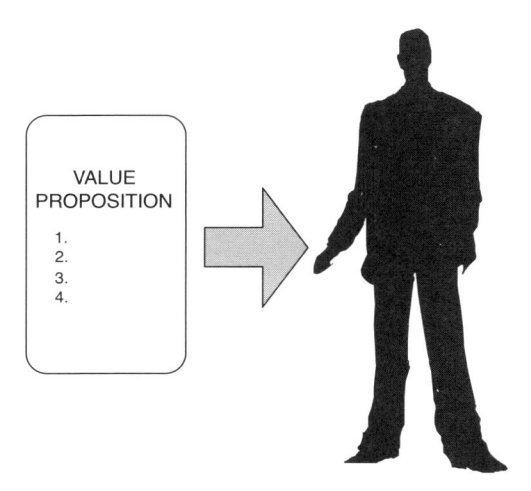

Figure 6-8: *Your value proposition must appeal to the "right" customer*

5. **Attack "with a flurry of blows."** The benefit of a simple attack strategy is that it's easy to *implement*. The downside is that it's probably easy to *oppose*.

Ninjas don't fight by the Queensberry rules; they do whatever it takes to win a fight. In the same way, you should aim to make your attack plan as hard as possible to "decode," copy, and counter.

Build your strategy in layers. Don't try to cram every possible action into the corporate-level page, or the marketing page. Ensure that value drivers, goals, and actions at various levels fit together and reinforce one another.

As Figure 6-9 shows, the basic elements of any product or service – functionality, quality, accessibility, and price – are just the start in creating a "total onslaught." There's any number of other things you can do to make your presence felt in the marketplace, to attract and lock in customers, and to fight off competitors.

A good marketing plan is, more accurately, a good business plan. It embraces every activity in your organization. For most businesses, there are more opportunities to do better than anyone imagines. All it takes is a little thought to see the possibilities.

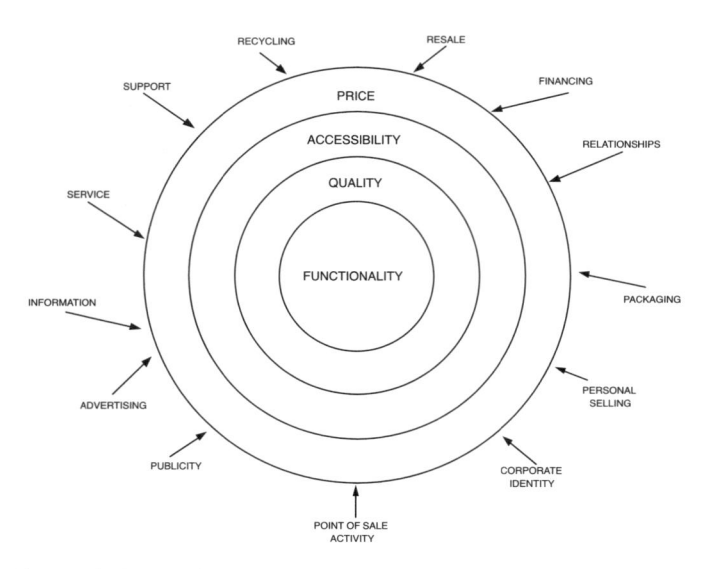

Figure 6-9: *Many marketing possibilities*

6. **Make selling systematic.** Selling is crucial to any firm's success, yet all too often it's left to salespeople. Is that a problem? You bet!

   Given free reign, they decide whom to call on and when, and also what to say. They become the organization's window on the world, and interpreters of all that's happening out there. Their views are accepted almost without question.

   As if distorting reality and providing misleading opinions were not enough, they also fail to see all the ways in which they might bond with their customers. And for almost every firm the opportunities are great.

   If this sounds like an attack on salespeople, it's not. They perform a vital function. A lot of them are real professionals. But they do have to be managed. Sales are too important to be left to chance.

   As a starting point for a new strike on the market, consider the example of a sales cycle in Figure 6-10.[114] It would probably take you about 10 minutes

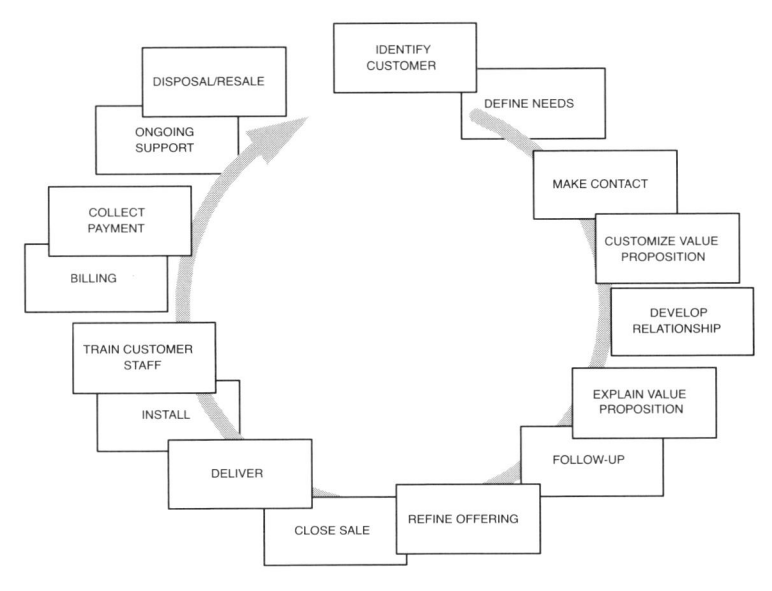

Figure 6-10: *The sales cycle*

to draw a similar picture for your own business. After that, you'd surely see many gaps in your current practices. Once again, your biggest challenge would be to trim your "to-do" list, so that you could focus on the high-impact possibilities.

It also pays to do the same analysis of *what the buyer goes through* (Figure 6-11). Again, this is sure to reveal many gaps in your strategy, as well as many opportunities for new sales. Most importantly, it highlights ways to build long-term relationships and "annuity" sales.

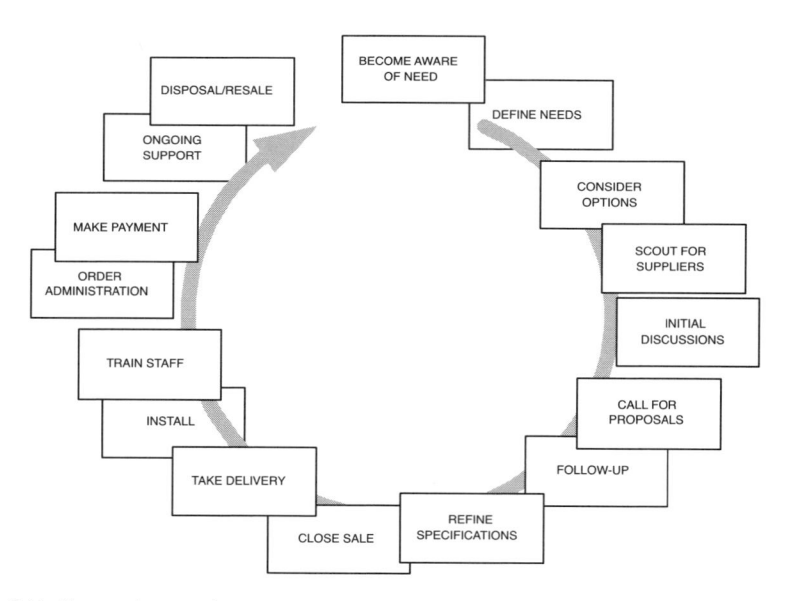

Figure 6-11: *The purchase cycle*

The next 30 days

There are many ways to get started on the journey towards value management – most of them costly and slow. Alternatively, you could get going *today*, and make rapid progress, probably without any extra costs. Simply:

- Follow the process I've outlined, with 30-day deadlines wherever possible;
- Spread the workload;
- Send people to see customers, or invite customers to come and spend time with your team;
- Set aside some chunks of time to brainstorm and create a new strategy;
- Follow up relentlessly and conduct robust progress reviews.

Can it really be as simple as that? There's only one way to find out. You have 30 days, and the clock is ticking.

7
MANAGEMENT MUST MANAGE!

"Value creation is the animating principle of modern management and its chief responsibility."

Joan Magretta with Nan Stone, *What Management Is*, 2002[115]

Value management can make a huge difference to most firms' results. But, as with all other business tools, there's an important rider:

First, *top* management must change.

A company's leaders must craft and manage a strategic conversation with value as its central theme. They must also walk their talk. They must demonstrate a personal commitment to doing what it takes to deliver value, and they must visibly *stop* doing whatever destroys value.

Value management isn't something you can announce and walk away from. It's not something you can hand to the HR department or a consultant.

Value management is a new "strategic conversation." It's another way of talking about your company, your goals, your actions, and your results.

This conversation must encourage everyone on your team to commit to creating shareholder value. It should instil discipline into everyday activities, while also inspiring people to constantly push the limits of performance. It's a task that's too important to hand over to anyone who cannot deliver on it.

Management is almost always the missing link when results fail to match expectations. Systems and processes are commonly undermined by executives who try to implement them without first accepting the need to change the way they behave themselves.

Corporate performance rests on the *management of people*. Get that wrong, and the finest system in the world is worthless. Get it right, and you probably don't need the finest system!

Every company needs to make value management an obsession for its people. *But the first obsession of top management must be people*. For they drive performance – and they can destroy it. Systems don't drive exceptional performance. Human beings do.

Why emphasize this? Because it's easy to put the cart before the horse. It happens with most of the interventions companies try. But it mustn't be allowed to happen if you're serious about value management. There's too much at stake.

The people factor

Many executives expect too little of their people, and underestimate their ability to make a difference. They talk about participation and empowerment, and muse about developing "leaders at every level." But, deep down, they're sceptical. They boast about having "the best people." But often they mean it only in a relative sense (other organizations have the real bozos). They talk about intellectual capital. But they are pretty sure it's not widely held.

This is how things are worldwide. It ensures that firms will underperform today and into the future.

Executives intent on delivering shareholder value cannot do it alone. They may make some smart decisions, but otherwise they're totally dependent on their people for results. They court disaster when they hold negative views about those people. Positive expectations can lead to extraordinary performance.

Your company cannot become world class with only a handful of stars. Not every employee has to be a star, but you do need a critical mass of people who volunteer their imagination and spirit to the cause.

Can all people do extraordinary things? Of course not. And many with great ability will disappoint you. But prejudging them is not smart. Instead, give them a chance to show their worth – along with all the resources and support they need – and then decide.

Value and values

If shareholder value is not the guiding principle in your company, everything else will crowd – and cloud – your agenda.

People at the top of an organization set the tone for the rest. By their words and actions, they define priorities and the boundaries of behaviour. Recent accounting scandals and lapses in corporate governance are all a symptom of managerial slack. When people behave badly, it's because they've been allowed to – or maybe even *encouraged* to. They have been tacitly or explicitly trained to act in a particular way.

As I noted in *Discovering the Essence of Leadership*, leaders at all levels create the space in which the people around them live their roles. If you want your team to manage for value, you have to provide a context in which they'll want to do that. Great performance doesn't come on its own. It must be inspired. You need *volunteers* with you.

The character of your organization is a consequence of people's beliefs and behaviours. If you leave it to define itself, it will. But the result may not be what you want. On the other hand, you can decide what kind of place you want your company to be, and you can influence its nature. The following questions will help you:
1. What assumptions guide us?
2. What turns us on?
3. What is not negotiable?
4. How do we behave?

Having agreed on the answers, you need to make it clear that they're not up for constant second-guessing and debate. There can be no "ifs" and "buts" about these matters. While flexibility is a crucial trait for any organization, *inflexibility* about its character is a must.

Context and content

Workers around the world have become suspicious of managers' motives. Reengineering was supposed to be a process by which companies redesigned their business models. In fact, many just hacked costs, and the first cost to go was usually "headcount." The slogan "don't automate – obliterate" became code for shedding jobs. Seldom did it lead to firms finding better ways of doing things.

When you start talking about value management, your people are likely to sense trouble. All around them, they've watched companies engage in wave after wave of retrenchments. Not surprisingly, they interpret "shareholder value" as a crudely coded message that "you don't count."

This makes it hard to win their support for change, and all the more important that they understand not just *what* might need to change, but *why* it's necessary. So value management requires a fine balance of communication, with the emphasis first on *context* and then on *content*.

One step at a time

No company can do everything immediately (though, under pressure, you may be tempted to try). First, you don't have the resources. You have to build or acquire them, and both take time. Second, you have to put in place the foundations of success.

However anxious you are to start showing results fast, you have to face this reality: building a business is a painstaking process. Though boldness is vital, "baby steps" should be the rule.

Imagine where you want to be in, say, three years from today. Now, create a "strategy staircase" to show what you must do in each of those three years. This clarifies your priorities and puts tasks in their proper order.[116] It also helps your team see both the big picture and the need to make each building block solid (Figure 7-1).

Now ask, "What few things must we do *this year*, to give us the best possible chance of getting there?" Then, "What must we do next year? And in year three?"

```
                              ┌─────────────────────────────┐
                              │         YEAR #3             │
              ┌───────────────┤                             │
              │    YEAR #2    │                             │
  ┌───────────┤               │                             │
  │  YEAR #1  │               │                             │
  │           │               │                             │
```

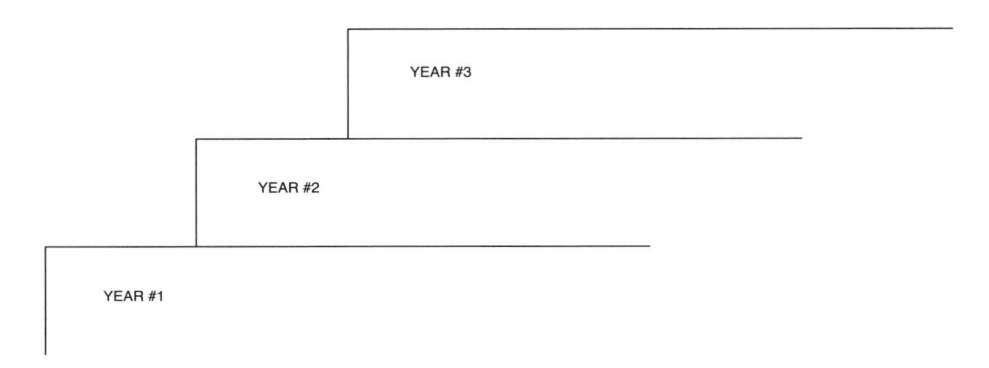

Figure 7-1: *The strategy staircase shows the way to the future*

To be effective, you have to get a few things right, then a few more. By laying a few "bricks" at a time, you create a sound foundation for the future. By "chunking" your work as projects, and sequencing their implementation, you can move relentlessly towards your bigger goals (Figure 7-2).

Every project must belong to a specific person and have a clear deadline. Even those that will take several months should have 30-day milestones. Reviews should be tough, to keep up the pressure for progress.

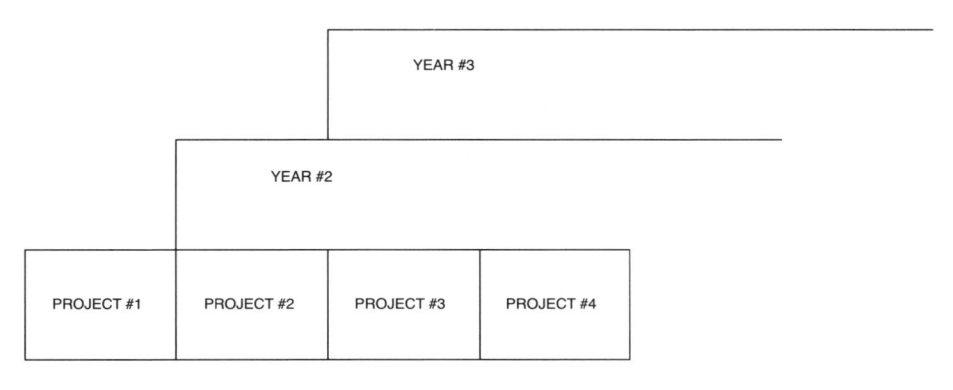

```
                         ┌─────────────────────────────────┐
                         │           YEAR #3               │
              ┌──────────┤                                 │
              │  YEAR #2 │                                 │
  ┌───────────┼──────────┼──────────┬──────────┐───────────┤
  │ PROJECT #1│PROJECT #2│PROJECT #3│PROJECT #4│
  └───────────┴──────────┴──────────┴──────────┘
```

Figure 7-2: *Projects are building blocks for achievement*

128 competing through value management

Maintaining momentum

When you introduce value management into your company, chances are you'll see remarkable improvements in very little time. In the early days, areas of weakness will be easy to spot. Fixing them will yield big rewards. Those of your people who come on board will be anxious to show they can make a difference.

Spotting opportunities will be equally easy, although seizing them might be hard and slow. Even small wins will be very motivational. A little praise and hype will go a long way.

But don't expect the first surge of excitement and achievement to last. Initial gains will give you cause to celebrate, but as the performance slope gets steeper, the sceptics will have plenty to say.

It's always easier to cut costs than add value, and the easiest way to cut costs is usually by eliminating jobs. So morale is likely to be a casualty. Fear may get a grip.

If this happens, people may assure you they're right behind you, when in fact they're hunkering in the trenches and hoping the whole nightmare will go away. So it's vital that you keep them focused on their goals, keep pushing for progress, and keep showing the benefits of what you're doing.

Great results are very motivating. So-so results are less of a turn-on. Struggling for minor improvements is a real turn-off. Most change initiatives face the reality of diminishing returns. Sustaining performance is a severe test of leadership.

When things slow down and you see less progress, you may be tempted to give up on the value management approach you've chosen, and try something else. If you feel this urge, fight it. Now is the time to push harder, not to waver.

Great performance doesn't come easy. Without perseverance it will be still-born. So you have to keep your team pushing forward, and encourage them to learn, innovate, and adapt.

The cycle of success

Personal character, management by walking around, and effective communication are all key factors in making this happen. Leadership is the ability to get results through other people. Contrary to popular myth, it's about being "hands on" rather than "hands off." You can't do it from afar. You can't get things done by remote control. Executing your strategy demands total involvement in the detail.

Empowerment is an important goal of value management. You want people to think for themselves, to respond sensibly to challenges, and to act as if they owned your company. But empowerment does not come through abdication. Paradoxically, it requires a lot of hand-holding.

Management by objectives fell from grace years ago. But every performance management method is a version of it. Many of them come with a huge increase in paperwork and meetings. They spawn bureaucracy.

Value management becomes "un-value" management when you let a system take over from good sense. If you're trying to get your people behind a vital new initiative – and if you want them to adopt it as their own – you need to get them excited by it. At the same time, those who choose to hold back, to drift, or to sabotage what you're doing must see that they can't win.

Companies don't manage themselves. Under-managing is as bad as over-managing. So you need to strike a balance between giving people space to do their own thing, and holding them to account for meaningful results.

The surest way to do it is by providing a forum in which to report results and share ideas, and by committing your company to disciplined debates in "ValuePlan forums" (Figure 7-3) that will achieve five things:

1. Make feedback on performance regular, so people know they're up against tight deadlines;
2. Let them report their progress, and talk about both their failures and successes;
3. Challenge their assumptions and their strategic thinking;
4. Make learning from each other *deliberate* rather than something that happens by *default*;
5. Give them the encouragement and mutual support they need to keep going.

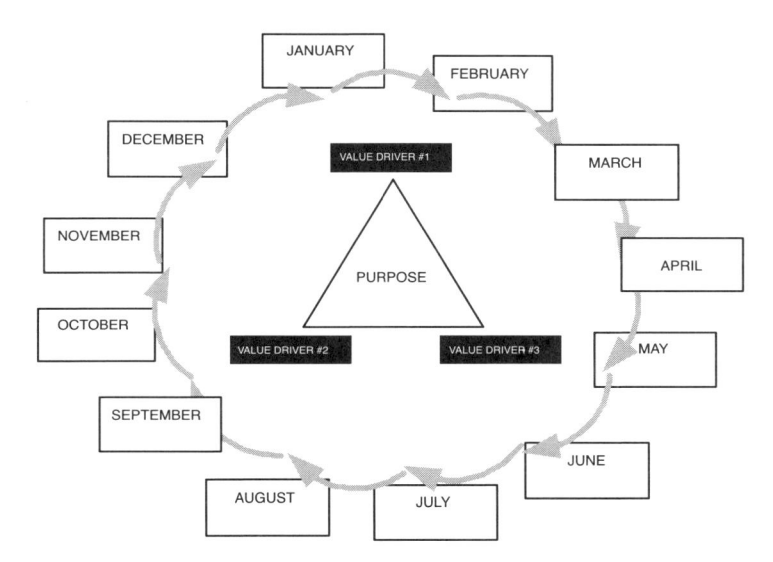

Figure 7-3: *The value management cycle*

Like much else in these pages, this is not a complicated idea. In fact, it's just a series of meetings, scheduled well in advance, with clear agendas. General Electric uses such an approach – it's known as their "social operating system" – and believes so strongly in it that the firm boasts about it in its annual reports and on its website (www.ge.com).

Who should attend these meetings?

You might invite the same people to be at all of them. Or perhaps it would be better to have a core group every time, with other people included according to the issue at hand. One or more sessions, for example, might focus on strategy, while others put quality or people matters in the spotlight. Operations must always be evident.

The important thing is that these forums shouldn't become boring "talk shops" in which the same people sound off every time about the same things. Everyone should be there for a purpose: to report, to share ideas, and to learn. Every meeting should add new impetus to your value management process.

Whatever the subject matter, the same rules should apply to each of these meetings. Here they are:
1. Delegates should know the agenda well in advance, and should come prepared;
2. Time-wasting and excuses are not acceptable;
3. The "strategic conversation" should be robust – direct and open, but always respectful;
4. Focus on getting results, on moving things forward;
5. Share learning.

CONCLUSION

In the age of "triple bottom line" reporting, managers can easily confuse themselves and their teams. What are the priorities? Where should people focus their efforts and resources? How should performance be measured? Without a clear point of view about what matters most, everything screams for attention; it's impossible to make trade-offs.

To complicate things further, "value" means different things to different people. So "creating value" means whatever they want it to mean.

Value management is based on a simple premise:

Maximum returns for minimal input.

That, in turn, means:
1. Economic profit is the No. 1 purpose of business;
2. Shareholder interests come first;
3. "Votes" of other stakeholders must be won to enable the firm to deliver on its purpose and survive over time;
4. Managers must concentrate resources on the few high-impact issues that will make the most difference – the 80/20 rule works in the firm's favour;
5. Managers must aim for rapid change, so learning takes place;
6. Every activity must aim for "value up, costs down."

How does your company rate against these criteria? Is everyone – in every function – working towards them? If not, you need to urgently refocus their efforts.

A simple set of metrics is essential. You need to decide on them soon, and communicate them widely and continually. But never forget that *measures* are no substitute for *management*. Or that value management is first and foremost about managing.

It's a logical process of deciding priorities and focusing resources. It involves everything your company does and the way you do everything. This is unquestionably a big task – and more urgent than you imagine. Fortunately, however, getting started is less difficult than it's made out to be.

A journey of growth and renewal

All business is risky. Many employees don't understand this. You need to educate them in the realities and complexities of survival and growth. That way, they'll see the meaning in their work. Fewer of them will be surprised when today's great product becomes tomorrow's dog, or when sales hit a wall because the economy slows. They'll also learn that:
- No matter how thoroughly you analyse the future, you will be surprised;
- Changing course – and *revisiting commitments* – is the smart thing to do in the face of new challenges;
- Judgement demands both hard facts and a healthy dose of gut feel;
- Goalposts have to be moved.

In a world of surprises, value management is only partly about getting things right. It's largely about learning and changing when you get them half right, and recovering when you get them badly wrong.

Value management is less about 20/20 *foresight* than about being able to cultivate and use *insights*. It's about creating space for constant experimentation, rapid adaptation, and growth in both individuals and teams.

If there's one characteristic that will distinguish tomorrow's business model from today's, it's *flexibility*. The ability to sense new possibilities, reconfigure your assets and capabilities, and set off in a new direction is worth a fortune. Keep this in mind when you consider the management tools you'll use. Be sure that the ones you choose don't cause precisely the problems you want to avoid.

Value management doesn't happen because you say it should or because you flood your company with graffiti. There is no "plug and play" path to success. All the sophisticated information technology or paperwork in the world is no substitute for "in your face," hands-on management.

There is no alternative to visible, vociferous leadership. Results don't come from sending instructions via e-mail, memo, or the message board. Nor do they come when leaders try to stay aloof and systematically "cascade their messages through the channels." *Personal contact is essential*. You have to be the missionary bearing your own message.

Value management is about both attitudes and actions. It's about doing the right thing, in the best way, as well as possible, to create maximum value for all your stakeholders.

The journey begins every day.

REALITIES

- **Value management is first and foremost about people.** Its purpose is to focus their energies, enable them to achieve extraordinary things, and inspire them to stretch towards their potential.

- **You have to start with strategy.** If you chase the wrong customers, if your value proposition doesn't appeal to them, if your business model is inappropriate, and if you can't make things happen, you're in trouble.

- **Measuring things only makes a difference when you *talk* about what you're measuring.** The most sophisticated metrics in the world are worthless without conversation. What gets measured does get managed, but it's only *what gets talked about* that will be either measured or managed.

- **There is no "one best way."** What works for one firm won't necessarily work for another. Metrics that are useful in one company – or one division or department – may not help elsewhere. You need to be flexible in applying them.

- **If you don't keep things simple, complexity will overwhelm you.** Too many measures, too much paperwork, and too many meetings will bring your company to a dead stop. Simplicity is a powerful weapon.

- **It's better to do a few key things brilliantly than many things quite well.** Focus! Focus! Focus!

- **You need to balance "the big picture" with fine-grained detail.** You have to keep your people focused on "the hill." At the same time, they need to know what small steps to take to get there, how they're progressing, and what they need to adjust or change.

- **The process must evolve to suit your firm's circumstances.** Different metrics will be useful at different times. Consider both external environmental conditions and the current state and needs of your firm. In a time of rapid growth, you'll want to focus on certain issues. An economic slump will bring different pressures.
- **People must see the process as fair and transparent.** Trust is a critical factor in performance management. It's hard to build and easy to kill. So be careful what information you hide.

READING

George A. Aragon, *A Manager's Complete Guide to Financial Techniques*, New York: The Free Press, 1982

Eleanor Bloxham, *Economic Value Management*, New York: John Wiley & Sons, 2003

Larry Bossidy and Ram Charan, *Execution*, New York: Crown Business, 2002

Ram Charan and Noel M. Tichy, *Every Business Is a Growth Business*, New York: Times Business, 1998

Tom Copeland, Tim Koller, and Jack Murrin, *Valuation*, Third edition, New York: John Wiley & Sons, 2000

Hugo Dixon, *Finance Just in Time*, New York: Texere, 2000, 2001

Peter F. Drucker, *Managing for Results*, London: William Heinemann, 1964

Robert G. Eccles, Robert H. Herz, E. Mary Keegan, and David M.H. Philips, *The Value Reporting Revolution*, New York: John Wiley & Sons, 2001

Al Ehrbar, *EVA: The Real Key to Creating Wealth*, New York: John Wiley & Sons, 2001

Kenneth R. Ferris and Barbara S. Pécherot Petitt, *Valuation: Avoiding the Winner's Curse*, New Jersey: Financial Times Prentice Hall, 2002

Louis V. Gerstner Jr., *Who Says Elephants Can't Dance?*, New York: HarperBusiness, 2002

H. Thomas Johnson and Robert S. Kaplan, *Relevance Lost*, Boston: Harvard Business School Press, 1987

Robert S. Kaplan and David P. Norton, *The Balanced Scorecard*, Boston: Harvard Business School Press, 1996

Robert S. Kaplan and David P. Norton, *The Strategy-Focused Organization*, Boston: Harvard Business School Press, 2001

James A. Knight, *Value Based Management*, New York: McGraw-Hill, 1998

Bartley J. Madden, *CFROI Valuation*, Oxford: Butterworth-Heinemann, 1999, 2000

Tony Manning, *Discovering the Essence of Leadership*, Cape Town: Zebra Press, 2002

Tony Manning, *Making Sense of Strategy*, Cape Town: Zebra Press, 2001; New York: Amacom Books, 2002

John D. Martin and J. William Petty, *Value Based Management*, Harvard Business School Press, 2000

James M. McTaggart, Peter W. Kontes, and Michael C. Mankins, *The Value Imperative*, New York: The Free Press, 1994

Lynn Sharp Paine, *Value Shift*, New York: McGraw-Hill, 2003

Alfred Rappaport, *Creating Shareholder Value*, New York: The Free Press, 1986

Alfred Rappaport and Michael J. Mauboussin, *Expectations Investing*, Boston: Harvard Business School Press, 2001

Joel M. Stern and John S. Shiely with Irwin Ross, *The EVA Challenge*, New York: John Wiley & Sons, 2001

G. Bennett Stewart III, *The Quest for Value*, New York: HarperBusiness, 1991

Bob Vause, *The Economist Guide to Analysing Companies*, Third edition, London: *The Economist* in conjunction with Profile Books, 2001

Jack Welch with John A. Byrne, *Jack: Straight from the Gut*, New York: Warner Books, 2001

REFERENCES

1. H. Thomas Johnson and Robert S. Kaplan, *Relevance Lost*, Boston: Harvard Business School Press, 1987
2. Charles A. O'Reilly III and Jeffrey Pfeffer, *Hidden Value*, Boston: Harvard Business School Press, 2000
3. Peter F. Drucker, *Managing for Results*, London: William Heinemann, 1964
4. Tony Manning, *Making Sense of Strategy*, Cape Town: Zebra Press, 2001; New York: Amacom Books, 2002
5. Tony Manning, *Discovering the Essence of Leadership*, Cape Town: Zebra Press, 2002
6. David L. Wenner and Richard W. LeBer, "Managing for shareholder value – from top to bottom, *Harvard Business Review*, November–December 1989
7. Christopher D. Ittner and David F. Larcker, "Innovations in performance measurement: trends and research implications," *Journal of Management Accounting Research*, Vol. 10, 1998
8. Robert G. Eccles and Nitin Nohria, *Beyond the Hype*, Boston: Harvard Business School Press, 1992
9. Kevin A. Hassett and James K. Glassman, *Dow 36,000*, New York: Times Books, 1999
10. David and Tom Gardner, *Rule Breakers, Rule Makers*, New York: Simon & Schuster, 1999
11. Jane M. Folpe, "Fortune's 50 most powerful women," *Fortune*, 25 October 1999
12. "Slip sliding away," *Business Week International*, 12 June 2000
13. Katrina Brooker, "Back to being Amazon.bomb," *Fortune*, 26 June 2000
14. Patricia Nakache, "Joe Blow StakesHisClaim.com," *Fortune*, 7 June 1999
15. Joseph Nocera, "Do you believe?" *Fortune*, 7 June 1999
16. Karen Lowry Miller, "The giants stumble," *Newsweek*, 8 July 2002
17. "America's amazing expansion," *The Economist*, 5 February 2000
18. Simon London, "Boards struggle to kick high-risk habits," *Financial Times*, 17 February 2003
19. Randy Myers, "Metric wars," *CFO Magazine*, October 1996
20. Randy Myers, "Measure for measure," *CFO Magazine*, 1 November 1997
21. John D. Martin and J. William Petty, *Value Based Management*, Harvard Business School Press, 2000
22. Alix Nyberg and Bill Birchard, "On further reflection," *CFO Magazine*, 1 March 2001
23. Philippe Haspeslagh, Tomo Noda, and Fares Boulos, "Managing for value: it's not just about the numbers," *Harvard Business Review*, July–August 2001

24. P. Haspeslagh, T. Noda, and F. Boulos, "Are you (really) managing for value?" INSEAD Working Paper, 2000/67/SM
25. "Scholars establish accounting framework for measuring 'economic value added,'" *Stanford Report*, 12 June 2002
26. Larry Bossidy and Ram Charan, *Execution*, New York: Crown Business, 2002
27. Bruce D. Henderson, *Henderson on Corporate Strategy*, Cambridge, Massachusetts: Abt Books, 1979
28. Gordon Donaldson and Jay W. Lorsch, *Decision Making at the Top*, New York: Basic Books, 1983
29. "How to live long and prosper," *The Economist*, 8 May 1997
30. Amar V. Bhidé, *The Origin and Evolution of New Business*, New York: Oxford University Press, 2000
31. Arie de Geus, *The Living Company*, Boston: Harvard Business School Press, 1997
32. James E. Post, Lee E. Preston, and Sybille Sachs, "Managing the extended enterprise," *California Management Review*, Vol. 45, No. 1, Fall 2002
33. P. Haspeslagh, T. Noda, and F. Boulos, 2000
34. Peter F. Drucker, "The information executives truly need," *Harvard Business Review*, January–February 1995
35. Sidney Schoeffler, Robert D. Buzell, and Donald F. Heany, "Impact of strategic planning on profit performance," *Harvard Business Review*, March–April 1974; Robert D. Buzell and Bradley T. Gale, *The PIMS Principles*, New York: The Free Press, 1987
36. Robert H. Hayes and William J. Abernathy, "Managing our way to economic decline," *Harvard Business Review*, July–August 1980
37. Gordon Donaldson and Jay W. Lorsch, 1983
38. Richard Foster and Sarah Kaplan, *Creative Destruction*, New York: Currency Doubleday, 2001
39. Clayton M. Christensen, *The Innovator's Dilemma*, Boston: Harvard Business School Press, 1997
40. Philip Stephens, "The world must learn to live with the reality of insecurity," *Financial Times*, 31 January 2003; " A century of progress," *The Economist*, 15 April 2002
41. Carol J. Loomis, "The 15% delusion," *Fortune*, 5 February 2001
42. Berkshire Hathaway annual report, 2001
43. Justin Fox, "Profits, Darwinism, and the Internet," *Fortune*, 6 March 2000
44. "Reasons for cheer," *Financial Times*, 5/6 October 2002
45. "The unfinished recession," *The Economist*, 28 September 2002
46. Chuck Lucier, Eric Spiegel, and Rob Schuyt, "Why CEOs Fall," *Strategy + Business*, Issue 28, Third Quarter 2002
47. Michael Hammer, "Forward to basics," *Fast Company*, November 2002
48. Jagdish Sheth and Rajendra Sisodia, *The Rule of Three*, New York: The Free Press, 2002
49. Sidney Schoeffler, Robert D. Buzell, and Donald F. Heany, 1974
50. Richard Minter, *The Myth of Market Share*, New York: Crown Business, 2002

51. George Stalk Jr., David K. Pecaut, and Benjamin Burnett, "Breaking compromises," 1997, in Carl W. Stern and George Stalk Jr., Eds., *Perspectives on Strategy*, New York: John Wiley & Sons, 1998
52. See the Bain Consulting firm's annual survey of management tools, at www.bain.com
53. Denis Higgins, *The Art of Writing Advertising*, Chicago: Advertising Publications Inc., 1965
54. Jeremy Hope and Robin Fraser, "Who needs budgets?" *Harvard Business Review*, February 2003
55. Michael C. Jensen, "Paying people to lie," Harvard Business School working paper 01-072, 2001
56. Tony Manning, *Making Sense of Strategy*, 2001, 2002; *Discovering the Essence of Leadership*, 2002
57. Tony Manning, *Making Sense of Strategy*, 2001, 2002
58. Jack Welch with John A. Byrne, *Jack: Straight from the Gut*, New York: Warner Books, 2001
59. Tony Manning, *Discovering the Essence of Leadership*, 2002
60. Robert S. Kaplan and David P. Norton, *The Balanced Scorecard*, Boston: Harvard Business School Press, 1996
61. Christopher D. Ittner, David F. Larcker, and Marshall W. Meyer, "Subjectivity and the weighting of performance measures: the evidence from a balanced scorecard," working paper, the Wharton School, University of Pennsylvania, 1997
62. Arthur M. Schneiderman, "Time to unbalance your scorecard," *Strategy + Business Briefs*, 23 October 2001
63. www.apqc.org
64. Orit Gadiesh and James L. Gilbert, "Transforming corner-office strategy into frontline action," *Harvard Business Review*, May 2001
65. Orit Gadiesh and James L. Gilbert, May 2001
66. Orit Gadiesh and James L. Gilbert, May 2001
67. Jack Welch with John A. Byrne, 2001
68. Arthur M. Schneiderman, 2001
69. Arthur M. Schneiderman, 2001
70. Alex Taylor III, "How Toyota defies gravity" *Fortune*, 8 December 1997
71. The Boeing Company annual report, 2001
72. David Batstone, "What's it worth?" *Business 2.0*, November 1998
73. Arthur M. Schneiderman, "Why balanced scorecards fail," *Journal of Strategic Performance Management*, January 1999
74. John Seely Brown and Paul Duguid, *The Social Life of Information*, Boston: Harvard Business School Press, 2000
75. Christopher D. Ittner and David F. Larcker, 1998
76. Eleanor Bloxham, *Economic Value Management*, New York: John Wiley & Sons, 2003; Christopher D. Ittner and David F. Larcker, 1998; John Dearden, "The case against ROI control," *Harvard Business Review*, May–June, 1969; John D. Martin and J. William Petty, 2000
77. Christopher D. Ittner and David F. Larcker, 1998
78. Anita M. McGahan and Michael E. Porter, "What do we know about variance in

accounting profitability?" *Management Science*, Vol. 48, No. 7, July 2002

79. Kris Bruckner, Stephan Leithner, Robert McLean, Charlie Taylor, and Jack Welch, "What is the market telling you about your strategy?" *McKinsey Quarterly*, No. 3, 1999

80. Harris Collingwood, "The earnings game," *Harvard Business Review*, June 2001

81. Laurence Booth, "What drives shareholder value?" paper presented to the Federated Press "Creating shareholder value" conference, 28 October 1998

82. Alfred Rappaport and Michael J. Mauboussin, *Expectations Investing*, Boston: Harvard Business School Press, 2001

83. Tom Copeland, Tim Koller, and Jack Murrin, *Valuation*, Third edition, New York: John Wiley & Sons, 2000

84. Charles Baden-Fuller and John M. Stopford, *Rejuvenating the Mature Business*, Boston: Harvard Business School Press, 1994; P.A. Geroski and P. Gregg, *Coping With Recession*, Cambridge: Cambridge University Press, 1997; G. Hawawini, V. Subramanian, and P. Verdin, "Is profitability driven by industry- or firm-specific factors? A new look at the evidence," INSEAD Working Paper, 2000/80/FIN

85. Michael J. Mauboussin, "Plus ça change, plus c'est pareil," CS First Boston, 13 December 1995

86. Christopher D. Ittner, David F. Larcker, and Marshall W. Meyer, 1997; Michael C. Jensen, "Value maximization, stakeholder theory, and the corporate objective function,"

Amos Tuck School of Business, Working paper no. 01-09, October 2001

87. Richard F.C. Dobbs and Timothy M. Koller, "The expectations treadmill," *The McKinsey Quarterly*, 1998, No. 3; Pablo Fernández, "EVA, Economic profit and cash value added do not measure shareholder value creation," IESE Business School paper, 22 May 2001; Charles E. Lucier and Amy Asin, "Toward a new theory of growth," *Strategy + Business*, First quarter 1996; Gary C. Biddle, Robert M. Bowen, and James S. Wallace, "Evidence on EVA®," *Journal of Applied Corporate Finance*, Vol. 12, No. 2, Summer 1999

88. "Shareholder value," *The Economist*, 25 January 2001

89. Kenneth R. Ferris and Barbara S. Pécherot Petitt, *Valuation: Avoiding The Winner's Curse*, New Jersey: Financial Times Prentice Hall, 2002

90. Thomas A. Stewart, *The Wealth of Knowledge*, New York: Currency, 2001

91. Alan M. Webber, "New math for a new economy," *Fast Company*, February 2000

92. John Dearden, "The case against ROI control," *Harvard Business Review*, May–June, 1969

93. H. Thomas Johnson and Robert S. Kaplan, 1987

94. Michael J. Mauboussin, "Thoughts on valuation," Credit Suisse First Boston Corporation, 21 October 1997

95. Tom Copeland and Jack Martin, *Valuation: Measuring and Managing the Value of Companies*, Second edition, New York: John Wiley & Sons 1994

96. Peter R. Fisher, "Restoring investor confidence: the key is disclosure," speech to The Securities Industry Association, Boca Raton, Florida, 8 November 2002
97. Message from Warren Buffett, Berkshire Hathaway annual report, 1999
98. Hugo Dixon, *Finance Just in Time*, New York: Texere, 2000, 2001
99. Peter F. Drucker, 1995
100. Michel E. Porter, "The importance of being strategic," *Balanced Scorecard Report*, March–April 2002
101. John Kay, *Foundations of Corporate Success*, Oxford: Oxford University Press, 1993
102. Alfred Rappaport, *Creating Shareholder Value*, New York: The Free Press, 1986
103. Gordon Donaldson, *Managing Corporate Wealth*, New York: Praeger Publishers, 1982
104. Christopher D. Ittner, David F. Larcker, and Taylor Randall, "Performance implications for strategic performance measurement in financial services firms," Social Science Research Network, March 2003
105. Brian Pitman, "Leading for value," *Harvard Business Review*, April 2003
106. Michael C. Jensen, 2001
107. Jeanie Daniel Duck, *The Change Monster*, New York: Crown Business, 2001
108. Tony Manning, *Making Sense of Strategy*, 2001, 2002; *Radical Strategy*, Johannesburg: Zebra Press, 1997
109. Noel M. Tichy and Ram Charan, *Every Business Is a Growth Business*, New York: Times Business, 1998
110. Orit Gadiesh and James L. Gilbert, "Profit pools: a fresh look at strategy," *Harvard Business Review*, May 1998
111. Michael Treacy and Fred Wiersema, *The Discipline of Market Leaders*, New York: Addison-Wesley Publishing Company, 1995
112. Fred Crawford and Ryan Matthews, *The Myth of Excellence*, New York: Crown Business, 2001
113. Tony Manning, 1997
114. Sandra Vandermerwe, *Customer Capitalism*, London: Nicholas Brealey Publishing, 1999
115. Joan Magretta with Nan Stone, *What Management Is*, New York: The Free Press, 2002
116. P. Williamson and M. Hay, "Strategic staircases," *Long Range Planning* 24, No. 4, 1991; Mehrdad Baghai, Stephen Coley, and David White, *The Alchemy of Growth*, London: Orion Publishing Group, 1999